Two mums' take on life with kids

I0345690

# Mum's the Word

Lis Norman & Tracey Samios

Copyright © 2016 Lis Norman and Tracey Samios

All rights reserved. No part of this book may be used or reproduced by any means, graphic, electronic, or mechanical, including photocopying, recording, taping or by any information storage retrieval system without the written permission of the copyright owner except in the case of brief quotations embodied in critical articles and reviews.

Making Magic Happen books may be ordered through online booksellers or by contacting:
www.makingmagichappenacademy.com

Because of the dynamic nature of the Internet, any web addresses or links contained in this book may have changed since publication and may no longer be valid. The views expressed in this work are solely those of the authors and do not necessarily reflect the views of the publisher and the publisher hereby disclaims any responsibility for them.

The author(s) of this book do not dispense medical advice or prescribe the use of any technique as a form of treatment for physical, emotional, or medical problems without the advice of a physician, either directly or indirectly. The intent of the author(s) is only to offer information of a general nature to help you. In the event you use any of the information in this book for yourself, which is your constitutional right, the author(s) and the publisher assume no responsibility for your actions.

ISBN: (sc) 978-0-9953976-6-8
ISBN: (e) 978-0-9946337-6-7

# DEDICATION

This book is dedicated to our kids, whose very existence created the memories that make up this book!

To Daniel and Callan-
I love you to the moon and back… infinity times and beyond! Thank you for being such amazing kids, enriching our lives in so many ways and editing and proofreading!

To Kathleen, Millie and Louise-
I love each of you deeply and marvel at the beautiful young women you have become; our lives have been blessed with your presence.

And of course to our beloved husbands…

Stu-
I loved you yesterday and I love you still. I will love you tomorrow and I always will. Thanks for the last 34 years of memories (both before and after kids!)

Ray-
You are my very precious partner in life, I love you very much.

A special thanks to Chris Norman (Bandits&Co) for the photography and design of front cover.

# INTRODUCTION

Being a Mum is the hardest job you will ever have. The hours are long (24/7!), the work is often tedious and repetitive, and you can *never* resign! The bonuses, however, make it all worthwhile; the small hand that curls itself in yours, the cuddles and kisses, and the words "I love you, Mummy" that have melted the hearts of mums worldwide. It is by far the most rewarding job you will ever hold, and it is yours forever.

This is a collection of stories and memories from life with our kids. It will show you how parenting can be very different from family to family. It may make you cry, we hope it makes you laugh, but most of all we hope it shows you there is no such thing as the perfect parent. As long as you and your kids are happy, you're doing okay!

Lis & Tracey

# CONTENTS

| | |
|---|---|
| Best friends | 5 |
| The Magic of childhood | 6 |
| Conception | 9 |
| Pregnancy | 12 |
| Hospital | 14 |
| Breastfeeding (Tracey) | 18 |
| Breastfeeding (Lis) | 20 |
| Mum's freedom | 22 |
| A dummy's guide to dummies | 24 |
| Time (Tracey) | 27 |
| Time (Lis) | 29 |
| Trauma of toilet training | 31 |
| In sickness and in health | 34 |
| Flour | 37 |
| Feeding time at the zoo | 39 |
| Hard to swallow | 42 |
| Humpty Dumpty | 44 |
| Night terrors | 46 |
| Night owl | 49 |
| Locked out | 51 |
| In the genes | 53 |
| Living in the moment | 56 |
| Kids on wheels | 58 |
| Little fingers | 61 |

| | |
|---|---|
| Naughty and nice | 63 |
| Activities (Tracey) | 65 |
| Activities (Lis) | 67 |
| A shopper is born | 70 |
| Collections | 72 |
| Recollections and collections | 74 |
| Bad teacher | 76 |
| Nessie | 80 |
| High jinx | 82 |
| Little Monkey | 84 |
| Mummy's little helpers | 86 |
| Computer games (Tracey) | 87 |
| Computer games (Lis) | 89 |
| A hairy tale | 91 |
| Fishy business | 94 |
| Four legged friends | 96 |
| The Rainbow Bridge | 98 |
| Special friends | 100 |
| Odd socks | 103 |
| Sock horror | 105 |
| Birthdays | 107 |
| Mother's worry | 110 |
| Mummy politics | 113 |
| Nine Eleven | 116 |
| Road trip | 119 |
| That's where clouds come from | 122 |
| So much more than just a mum | 123 |
| Blow, blow, blow your nose | 127 |

| | |
|---|---:|
| Double double this this! | 130 |
| Mum knows best | 132 |
| Never ending eggs | 134 |
| Mum loses her temper | 136 |
| Eensie weensie spider | 138 |
| Boys will be boys | 141 |
| Race for the front seat | 143 |
| Planes, trains and automobiles | 145 |
| Pocket money | 148 |
| The Wiggles concert | 150 |
| The F bomb | 152 |
| Sleep | 154 |
| Belt up | 158 |
| Memories | 160 |
| Mother's Day | 162 |
| Daddy's little helpers | 164 |
| TV and DVDs | 166 |
| TV world | 168 |
| Trouble | 170 |
| What's that smell? | 172 |
| Venturing out | 174 |
| Yarram pool | 179 |
| Going once, going twice | 182 |
| The family home | 185 |
| The magic of Harry Potter | 188 |
| The little things | 191 |
| Toys "R" us | 193 |
| Trust | 195 |

| | |
|---|---|
| Everyone's a winner | 197 |
| Have a banana | 200 |
| Ode to my life partner | 202 |
| Revenge time | 204 |
| Me, myself and I | 206 |
| Family holidays | 208 |
| The Anzac on the Wall | 211 |
| Good guys don't always win | 215 |
| The circle game | 216 |
| Fifteen minutes of fame | 218 |
| Blast off | 221 |
| Visiting Lorraine's house | 224 |
| End | 226 |

# BEST FRIENDS

Tracey has been my best friend for almost fifty years and we share so many memories, both before and after kids. The following is an essay I wrote in a Year 11 exam (Form 5, as we knew it!) in which I wrote about our childhood memories. I think it's a perfect beginning to our memoir of motherhood memories, beginning our journey from kids to mums!

Lis Norman (left) & Tracey Samios.

# THE MAGIC OF CHILDHOOD (LIS)

I remember the day the magic died, but I'd rather remember when it was there.

Tracey was my best friend. I mean, she still is, but we've changed from the children we were; the children who played in those brief spaces between school and to whom everything was a dream. What little fuel it took to keep our dreams burning then.

I remember so many things, precious things from my childhood, things which over the years I have lost. For instance, the way I talked to my pet cat and dog; I can't talk to an animal the way I did then, I've tried. Tracey and I lived in our dream world, a world in which parents and animals were most important, and a dream in which the world was our oyster. I remember the way we used to cook, using soil and water for coffee (probably as good as I make now), daisy heads for eggs, and rocks for potatoes. Only we knew when those eggs and potatoes were cooked to perfection!

I remember the magical games of doctors and nurses, with our pet doll Anne the only patient. Over the years that doll suffered major changes with the most drastic being her acquisition of a rock for a heart during a major heart transplant operation!

I remember the cities we built in the sand, complete with roads and even shop signs, hexagons made from cardboard. Alas, however, the tide would eventually change, and the sea would inevitably wash away our cities, just as my childhood dreams would eventually be washed away.

The memory which hurts the most is the memory of the game of *"I'm going to be"* – what glamorous jobs we chose for ourselves; women spies with the precious secrets of our country safe in our head, on our way to China, a sinister man sitting across the aisle…

I remember, too, the tall ancient tree which had dominated our back garden. Looking at it now it's hard to believe that it had at one stage of my life been an entire jungle. Somehow over the years Tracey and I changed; our minds shifted into higher gear. No longer were we little girls with games on our minds, we were "big" girls with the latest boyfriends and the latest parties on our minds.

I remember the day the magic died. I came home from school one summer, went down to our playhouse, entered, and shut the door behind me. I sat down and waited for the old spells and the magic to begin. Nothing happened. Sadly, I looked down at the teacup in my hand, cracked and dusty. Somewhere far off a door slammed and a dog barked. Slowly I left, closing the door tightly behind me.

No longer was it the 'playhouse'; after that it was the 'storeroom,' used to store last year's dresses from the school dance, last year's hats, last year's jeans now outgrown.

Gradually my life became more and more demanding and more and more exciting, and I learnt to put the past behind me, but nothing could fill the small empty ache inside of me, which was all that remained of my childhood dreams.

I didn't ask Tracey how the magic died for her. I didn't want to know.

# CONCEPTION (LIS)

My journey to becoming pregnant was a long and often traumatic one. Once we decided to start our family, when the months rolled by without me getting pregnant, my husband and I had to accept the fact that we might need help. So began a roller coaster ride; fertility drugs, miscarriages, IVF, and ectopic pregnancies.

Becoming pregnant became the focus of our day to day life and it seemed that everywhere I looked there were pregnant women or friends (including Tracey), announcing an impending happy arrival. And then of course, everywhere you went the inevitable questions- *"Do you have kids?" "When are you going to start a family?"* Having married at 21 (who would marry that young?) these were perfectly natural questions for people to ask seven or eight years later, but they were questions I didn't want to have to deal with.

I've always said that if we knew there was going to be success at the end, the whole process would have been bearable. What was so hard was dealing with the fear that it would never happen. People constantly offered well-meaning advice; relax, don't drink, drink more, go on a holiday, forget about it, and so on…. until you felt like screaming (or strangling the advice giver!) My all-time personal favorite had to be "oh well, you don't really want kids, they're a pain in the neck…"

I won't dwell on this time except to say that the whole experience bought my husband and me closer together; something we were very grateful for, as often it can drive couples apart. We learnt to do many things, including giving myself daily injections in the stomach, and him having to give me one in the bum! Our whole lives revolved around the clock – I even had to get a pass out from a Bon Jovi concert, go to his nearby work, and lie on the floor for my injection. Luckily everyone else had left for the day! It's ironic that in our last successful attempt I dropped the vial of liquid used in the injection and watched it shatter on the tiles. I got a replacement vial at the mere cost of $150 and all was back on track. My conclusion – I bought 2 vials, therefore I got 2 babies!

Through all this I learnt that my husband truly is my 'soul-mate' and the last 32 years of marriage we have been through thick and thin and are still as much in love as when we first got married. (Before running for the bucket, don't worry, he still drives me insane at times, as I do him!)

After 10 eventful years of trying, I made the phone call (fittingly, it was my birthday) to see whether our last attempt had been successful, and I was given the best present ever;

"Yes, you are pregnant". Then 2 weeks later-"levels are high – it looks like twins."

"Are they twins?"

"No, the hospital was having a buy one get one free special!"

# PREGNANCY (LIS)

I absolutely loved being pregnant! I slept like a baby (stored it all in a sleep bank from which I would be making multiple withdrawals once the boys came along), lived on strawberry milk and frozen yoghurt, and couldn't touch coffee… I suffered mild morning sickness for the first few months, and then had a major fright when I started bleeding at ten weeks (apparently there were three embryos initially). The only other discomfort I recall was indigestion and then *indignation* when my husband failed to fulfil my craving for a McMuffin- apparently he arrived minutes after they stopped serving breakfast! I still tease him that he couldn't get me the only craving I had ever asked him for!

I can still remember the excitement of the first time I felt movement – there are no words to describe this feeling, the realisation that there is really a living being (or 2!) growing inside you.

Sadly my Mum suddenly passed away when I was seven months pregnant. She was so excited about the boys impending arrival and bored everyone she knew with daily updates. Her being in intensive care, her death, and her funeral all seemed very surreal, and are honestly a bit of a blur in my memory. I totally focused on my babies and that got me through.

Then at 8 months I was at the Grand Final with my Dad (he was an M.C.C Member) watching my beloved St. Kilda lose to Adelaide. Dad was convinced I was going to go into labour; maybe I should have – it would have saved me the grief of watching!

My last memory of being out and pregnant was probably at 37 weeks when I was shopping at Target. All of a sudden I was struck by overwhelming exhaustion, which led me to sitting on the floor in the children's section where I was. At the time I thought nothing of it – I was tired and needed to sit, but when I look back now I think how funny I must have looked, particularly when I was getting back up! There could have been a store announcement never before heard; "Customer assistance to Children's Wear – there's a beached whale!"

Finally 38 weeks arrived, and off to hospital bright and early we went – the first of many early wake-ups for YEARS to come!

"Each month has an average of 30 days. Except the last month of pregnancy which has 5,654 days!"

# HOSPITAL (LIS)

My hospital visit began with our arrival at the reception desk to book in. A classic case of my pregnancy brain (anyone who has been pregnant understands that term all too well) was the receptionist sarcastically asking "and what are you in for?" and me proceeding to tell her "the Maternity Section" - only to have my husband gently point out that with my stomach it was pretty obvious what I was there for!

I recall badly wanting a strawberry thick shake from the McDonald's, which was located next to the hospital, but of course I was fasting in preparation for my caesarean. I had visions of that cold thick shake sliding down my throat all morning! Finally the time came and off we went to operating theatre, and a theatre it was indeed, with a cast of many! There were doctors and nurses and medical students, and of course my darling husband; it strikes me as very strange how such a momentous occasion in our life was so mundane and matter of fact for others. To them, it was just another day on the job, whilst to us it was Miracle Day – the day we would finally get to meet our precious babies!

They reassured me that when the time came and the screen was lowered, I would have eyes only for my babies, and not my various bodily organs that would be on display! I was sceptical, but after having an epidural, desperately asking for something to throw up in, and feeling the most bizarre, very strong wrenching and pulling sensation on my insides, one baby was pulled free, followed two minutes later by the other- I saw nothing but those precious beings. I clearly remember crying and the interminable wait for them to be brought to me after everything was checked. And then they were in our arms, and life as a family began...

I had an irrational fear that I guess every Mum has while pregnant: that I wasn't going to love, or even like my babies, but, boy, was that ever time wasted worrying! The second I looked into those faces I was lost forever.

My hospital stay was not ideal, doubly so because we had twins. We were promised a night out together before going home (never happened), a relaxing bath with music of my choice (never happened), and a nurse to help at all times (never happened)! From the time we went back to our room we were overwhelmed with both visitors and information until our heads were swimming. Our babies were kept in the nursery overnight and I would go there to feed them.

The downside of this was that all the nurses would be busy running to other rooms to help Mums, leaving me quite often alone. This continued until the third night when, upon arrival at the nursery, the nurse told me that she would go and get 'Michael.' I tried to tell her I had twins, Daniel and Callan, but she wasn't listening! Finally I convinced her (after starting to doubt it myself) that I had two babies and she brought them to me and then promptly left. In the middle of the night, there I sat, with my two by now screaming babies, not knowing how on earth to feed them both. The dam broke; hysterical tears flooded –and when a nurse came back I lost it completely.

"My Mum just died, I can't feed my babies, and no one will help!"

Soon there were about six nurses gathered around me trying to calm me down. I think I should have done that on night one!

However worse was to follow; on the last night in hospital, when my husband would be staying there also, they said the babies would sleep in our room. That was, and to this day still remains, the worst night of our lives. Neither of us slept one wink with first one baby crying, and upon us having settled him, the second baby starting. Finally in desperation we rang for the nurse at 6AM and pleaded with her to take them back to the nursery. Imagine my sheer terror when we were told we were going home that morning! I thought we were never going to cope, let alone sleep ever again.

The car ride home was bizarre, with my husband driving at about 40km an hour. All of a sudden we had precious cargo on board and everything in our world had changed!

One happy memory of hospital I do cherish is proudly wheeling my double cot down the hallway and feeling like royalty. And that special unique "baby smell" that each baby has (strangely enough, one of mine had a far stronger one than the other); if you could bottle and sell it you would become an instant millionaire!

"Remember the day you bought me home and you were filled with love and joy? Go to that place because I just drew all over the walls!"

# BREASTFEEDING (TRACEY)

You would think that breastfeeding would be easy, part of the natural process of feeding and bonding with your baby, but, of course, it wasn't easy for me. For the first month of breastfeeding, my first child Kathleen had a ferocious appetite and was feeding every three hours. My breasts would become uncomfortably full with milk and began to leak into the absorbent breast pads held in my bra! Kathleen, ready for her feed, would latch on like a piranha, and cause me great pain. After a week I developed mastitis, which left me feeling like I had the flu with body aches, a headache and very painful cracked nipples. I was so desperate I even tried the old wives tale of placing refrigerated cabbage leaves over my breasts to relieve the pain! (The coolness did provide some relief.) I'm sure there is a photo of this lurking somewhere in a drawer just waiting to appear and embarrass me!

As the weeks progressed, the whole process of feeding Kathleen became tiring and daunting. I felt I was a failing mother and was just about to give up when I decided to get in touch with the local lactation nurse and made an appointment to go and see her. Her name was Flo, short for Florence (Nightingale), and I visited her at the local community centre that very afternoon. Flo showed me helpful feeding techniques to lessen the pain and give my breasts a chance to heal. My little girl was learning just as I was; it felt more enjoyable and made me feel more relaxed and confident. I was so glad that I had kept going and pushed through this temporary period of discomfort. Sometimes seeking professional help and guidance can be the perfect solution to your problem.

"Ready made with love!"

# BREASTFEEDING (LIS)

Breastfeeding was one of many things that I changed my ideas about when my babies became reality. I thought I was *never* going to feed both babies at once and feel like Bessie the Cow, but I soon realised that if I didn't, I would be feeding them non-stop! Luckily I never experienced any problems and apart from being thoroughly confused in the hospital with each different nurse giving me different advice, I found the whole process trauma free. It was one of the things that made me realise that babies aren't anywhere near as fragile as you imagine them to be; you try picking up two babies off the floor and attaching them when you're on your own and you'll soon see what I mean!

I was, for quite a while, referred to as 'the milk bar,' which, although amusing, doesn't do much for your self-esteem! I frequently sat in my rocking chair, feeding my babies and watching them fall asleep, full and content; this was a blissful chance to catch up on some much needed sleep, but invariably I would desperately need to go to the toilet – lucky for me I had great bladder control, and I guess it was one way of strengthening my pelvic floor! I had one mantra that I followed religiously- "Let sleeping babies lie."

I breastfed both boys for 8 months, then one went on the bottle as he was a 'grazer' and not getting enough. The other was a fast worker who was done in fifteen minutes or so.

I look back now and wonder how I did that, but at the time it was no big deal, and it remains one of my favourite recollections of their babyhood. I spent many hours studying those tiny faces as they fed; a very special time that will never be forgotten.

"Whoever said there was no use crying over spilled milk obviously never pumped 800 ml of it then accidentally knocked it over!"

# MUM'S FREEDOM (TRACEY)

After the birth of your first baby, your life changes forever. You go from *me* to *us* in a literal breath when your baby starts their life. Your entire psyche goes into shock- it takes time to get used to not putting yourself first ever again. Everyday actions like showering, eating, and sleeping are put behind your baby's needs. After getting used to these changes, you take on this new role of motherhood, and adapt and endeavour to do the best you can for all of your family.

I often found myself tired and weary, sometimes taking shortcuts with things like putting make-up on hurriedly and doing my hair in a matter of seconds. Life in general seemed such a rush as we raced around for Mothers Group get togethers, doctor's appointments, mother craft visits, birthday parties, Christenings and every other necessity and commitment in a baby's life. After your second child is born, you're armed and ready, and by the third you feel like a pro, and get on with the job of being super mum, an expert on all things in the world.

I remember one morning lying in bed at 6AM awaiting the onslaught of tiny feet coming to wake us. I thought "I need to cherish this time!" I knew it was only going to last for another few years, and that, exhausting as it was now, I would miss it when it stopped. As the girls grew older, the helping with dressing slowly dropped off, the brushing and putting their long hair up in a plait or braid slowly wore off, the preparation of food for them….actually, let's not go there! When they began their teenage years, you struggle with when you are ready to leave them at home and duck out to do the food shopping and other things. Each child is different and it's a turning point when you decide this can happen. It's amazing when the day finally arrives when all of them no longer rely on you for their every whim. It is very liberating to be able to hop in the car and leave them all at home and not worry about them. Even though it feels wonderful and you regain your personal freedom, it's also a very sad time- you miss the closeness of their reliance on you. All that said, I don't think I will ever stop hearing *"Mum, where are my socks?!"*

"I USED TO THINK HAPPY HOUR WAS AT 5PM. TURNS OUT IT IS THE HOUR BETWEEN YOUR KIDS GOING TO BED AND YOU GOING TO BED!"

# A DUMMY'S GUIDE TO DUMMIES! (LIS)

Another parenting aid that I was never going to use was a dummy. Of course, *my* baby was going to be the non crying variety; one that suckled contentedly, fell asleep peacefully, and woke with a mere whimper. Why would I need a dummy?

Then the reality of two crying babies and a sleep deprived me shattered that fantasy, leaving me desperately seeking ways of achieving peace. I turned to the dark side and purchased dummies (colour coded); a red and a blue for Twin 1, and a yellow and a white for Twin 2. (Much like Bananas in Pyjamas as B1 and B2, my babies were referred to by the medical profession as T1 and T2!) Colour coding became a part of day to day life as they grew older, with everything from baby bottles to lunch boxes. Finding things in different colours was sometimes a disadvantage with having twins, but generally with mine one had green and one had blue.

But back to the dummies; they calmed many an unhappy moment in our house and although at times they would cause grief when they popped out whilst sleeping, the fast trip to the room to put it back in, was to me vastly favourable over extended crying.

We took it that step further and did the unthinkable and dipped them in honey or jam, causing those little mouths to work overtime, sucking ferociously and gaining us bonus peace. This was our back up plan when we were out and needed to buy some extra time before all hell broke loose! I know many would be horrified, but it worked like a charm.

Like many things in life, the dummy makers decided to make the Normans' life harder, and stopped making the particular brand of dummy that we used. Vainly we drove all over Melbourne trying to find one, but to no avail. (Again, today it would have been an easier task with the Internet and the ability to buy online, even from overseas!) We tried other dummies but had no success; neither would take them. I was extremely apprehensive as time went on and the rubber grew thinner; I thought we were in for a torrid time when they finally split, but like so much in our family life, the expected did not happen. The broken dummy was revealed to them, the replacement refused, and off to sleep they went. Why is it that things you anticipate being difficult are quite often stress free, whilst the things you think you will sail through prove to almost be your undoing?

This is Parenting Rule Number One:

"Always expect the unexpected!"

We did manage to lose one of those precious dummies somewhere in our house, and to this day (some seventeen years and one major renovation later) it has never been found!

"Dummy squats: Act of picking up your child's dummy off the ground a million times a day!"

# TIME (TRACEY)

Before children, I used to sit and think about things and watch the world go by. I enjoyed my own company, shopping on my own and happily sitting in solitude drinking coffee in a café. People-watching intrigued me, and on a weekend I could do it for hours on end with nothing else demanding my attention.

You don't realise how free and unencumbered your life is before children. In one day, all this changes- the minute your first child enters the world you lose your own identity, and this tiny being becomes the centre of your universe. All of your senses are completely tuned to their every movement and sound. Free time becomes a distant memory, replaced by an overwhelming schedule of feeding, burping, nappy changing, prams, lifting and carrying around, washing, and little sleep. It's incredible how you adapt and cope in your new role as a mother and probably even more amazing that most mums choose to go through it all again, even knowing what's to come. I guess it's because a mum's love transcends all else.

"You know you're a mum when sleeping in until 8am is as magical as riding out of your bedroom on a unicorn!"

# TIME (LIS)

Nobody really understands the concept of time quite like a new mum. In the blink of an eye your time is no longer your own; instead you are a slave to your newborn. Your offspring are like the little creatures that eat at your time whilst you are playing computer games!

I look back now and wonder how it is I had no time for simple things such as plucking my eyebrows, having a bath, or reading a book – all things that both now and pre-children I take for granted. The days can seem so much longer than 24 hours, and yet the time that your baby sleeps seems over in the blink of an eye.

Routine and clock watching ruled my new world. No more spontaneity or playing by ear, life became regimented with a strict schedule to follow. Even my husband didn't quite understand the way that I felt; he went to work, and could clock off from baby world for a time. Time on your own became a much treasured thing; I remember him insisting on helping by putting out the washing and not quite understanding that I *really* wanted to do it alone. (I wish someone would offer to do it now!)

The irony was that every time I was apart from my precious babies, I missed them like crazy, and couldn't wait to be back with them!

"I recently had a major revelation since becoming a mother... I know why mamma bear's porridge was cold!"

# TRAUMA OF TOILET TRAINING (LIS)

Toilet training was an experience that I really wasn't looking forward to. I had visions of multiple changes of clothes, and sitting in the toilet all day (not my favourite location). I had never worried about changing nappies and had used a nappy wash service for quite some time before switching to disposables. I liked the security of going out and not having to find toilets or deal with 'accidents'. It was amazing how often the boys would dirty their nappies one after the other; I guess their bowels as well as their minds (yes, they often finish sentences of each other) are truly in sync.

At age two, I decided to bite the bullet and try a day without nappies. What a disaster! First one wet his pants, and then the other; change of clothes, and the same thing happened. Take three, and again the same result; I was fast running out of both jocks and patience, and abandoned the exercise.

Some six months later they both seemed ready and with a reward system in place (a snake lolly for a number two in the toilet and a few smarties for a successful pee) we tried again. Neither had been keen on sitting on a potty, so we skipped that and went straight to the big toilet with a kiddy seat. I bless the inventor of pull up pants; they were awesome when going out, and later for security overnight. Apart from the occasional abandoning of the supermarket trolley to take one to the toilet, and a tendency to "pretend wee" to get some smarties, the dreaded process was done with minimal fuss. My advice to all mums is to wait until your kids are ready (and every kid will be different) - who cares if it's a few months, or even a year later, than other kids?

I am very grateful that neither of my boys was a bed-wetter and over the years we only had one or two accidents.

My favourite story that I read in a Toddler Taming book was about a mum whose husband worked at a Sewage Plant. This mum would sit her son on the toilet and say "Pass a message down the pipe to dad!"

How to potty train a toddler in five easy steps:

1. Buy your favourite wine
2. Open wine
3. Pour wine
4. Drink wine
5. Repeat

# IN SICKNESS AND IN HEALTH (LIS)

My babies were very healthy babies, and we rarely had to visit the doctor. This continued (luckily) right through their childhood – so much so that when one was finally at the doctors at age 12, the doctor asked whether we usually went elsewhere. When I told her, no, we just hadn't been for a couple of years, she laughed and said the last time he'd been there was at age *two*! I can count on one hand the number of times they had gastro and they only suffered from the occasional cold. In fact, it was I who had been sick the most; when I first got home from hospital after giving birth I had the worst bout of gastro I had ever endured. I think it was a reaction to my overzealous washing of hands and increased hygiene! Then when they were still babies, on several occasions, I suffered dreadful migraines. They must have had some in-built sensor that was in tune with what I needed because on each occasion they slept longer than usual – me lying on the floor with an arm around each, praying that they would stay asleep.

The one major scare we had was at 18 months old when one developed bronchial pneumonia. I took him to the doctor, who sent me to the nearby emergency hospital for X-rays. No one seemed very perturbed by our arrival, all very casual, saying he didn't look too bad. I knew my babies though, and knew something was not right. The nurses had immediately pegged me as a neurotic mother; if they only knew how far from the truth that was. When we finally had the X-ray, suddenly everything changed… he needed to be admitted, and they didn't admit children at that particular hospital, so an ambulance was called to transport us. I went in the ambulance and my husband followed behind with the other twin. It was the night of a full moon, and thankfully they were in their 'moon obsessed' stage, so the ambulance ride was spent moon gazing. One of the paramedics asked if we had private health insurance and excitedly I said yes, thinking we would get preferential treatment or a private room- only to be told not to mention it whatever I did, as the treatment would be no different, but we'd get a bigger bill. So much for the health system! My little boy spent two nights in hospital, the first in an oxygen tent, me dozing fitfully in the chair next to him until the nurse took me to the playroom, where mattresses were laid on the floor for the mums. I had only been there a matter of minutes when there was a loud cracking sound, and the fish tank in the corner of the room exploded! Happily, I returned to his room where I kept vigil in the chair.

The next night was a nightmare; he was well on the road to recovery, but desperately missing his brother, and expressed this by crying uncontrollably for hours while I paced the corridors trying to soothe him. It was then that I fully realised the sheer strength of my boys' unfaltering deep connection. One nurse exasperatedly asked me what I did with him when he did this at home. She looked extremely sceptical when I informed her he'd never done this before. I told her to imagine if the person who had been by your side for your entire *life* was suddenly not there – I bet she'd be screaming too!

I have never been so pleased to get home and reunite my little treasures. The one positive that I did take from the whole experience was the kind doctor who said to me, "When mum is worried, I worry – mums know their babies best," and from then on I trusted my maternal instinct implicitly.

First child eats dirt. Parent calls doctor.

Second child eats dirt. Parent cleans out mouth.

Third child eats dirt. Parent wonders if she really needs to feed him lunch.

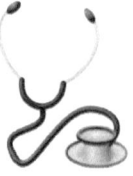

# FLOUR (TRACEY)

Back when my eldest, Kathleen, was three years old, bread makers were very popular, and we used to make our own bread. The smell of cooking bread wafting throughout the house made us drool in anticipation, and it tasted delicious!

We bought the ingredients for the bread in large quantities and stored them in the kitchen pantry. The flour was kept in a large, cylindrical container, on a shelf well out of little hands' way. One day I returned home after grocery shopping, having left Kathleen in her Dad's trusty care! I opened the door to hear the sounds of the vacuum (an instant giveaway that something was up) and my husband saying "Now Kathleen, we don't need to tell Mum about this, OK? "

He turned and upon seeing me smiled sweetly and innocently asked "What?" I quizzed him as to what had happened and discovered Kathleen had climbed on the pantry shelf and sent the flour container flying. It looked very much to me that Kathleen was spreading the flour further, and faster than Ray was vacuuming it up.

Quite often I would come home to similar scenes and every time

I went out I would anxiously wonder what would greet me on my return. Occasionally I would ring to check that everything was OK and my husband would respond with things like "Sure. Oh, by the way, where do we keep the band aids?" Hmm, good babysitters are hard to find!

"Once upon a time my house was clean. Then the kids woke up!"

# FEEDING TIME AT THE ZOO (LIS)

Feeding toddlers can be a tricky business! Mealtimes for my two were spent at a little wooden table and chairs, and this continued until they outgrew the chairs! Dinner together as a family was not an option, as Dad didn't get home until 7pm or later, so I would feed the boys first and then we would eat (often after they were in bed).

Their palate was pretty plain, but I figured (after many failed attempts at getting them to eat veggies) it was better to feed them what they liked and what I knew they would eat, than engage in a hopeless battle!

One of them would have lived on bread alone if I had let him, and the other loved tomatoes! This continued throughout his childhood and he would often grab a whole tomato from the fridge and eat it for his after school snack or polish off a punnet of cherry tomatoes!

Most of their meals in younger years consisted of sausages or chicken, and salad and copious amounts of fruit. They loved strawberries, grapes, watermelon, cantaloupe, kiwi fruit, apples, and bananas. Luckily both have Dad's metabolism and can eat like a horse and not gain any weight. Me on the other hand, I look at food and the weight goes on – totally unfair!

Both have a sweet tooth (like me) and I indulged them with treats of chocolate and soft drink (in moderation). I believed that if it was forbidden, when they had the chance they would overdo it; nothing is quite as tempting as forbidden fruit (or more to the point – chocolate).

I went through phases of scouring cooking books and trying to tempt them with different food but eventually stopped when I got sick of one liking it and one not and having to cook multiple meals in one night! The last straw was the day I spent all afternoon preparing a special meal for them, only to see their faces turn up when they ate it. It's a bittersweet memory though; Callan went and put his plate in the fridge, declaring, "It's just so yummy, Mummy, I'm going to save it for tomorrow!" I thought he could be destined for a bright future in politics; tell the people what they want to hear!

Toddler books are an invaluable resource for advice and when I read the words, "No toddler has starved from not eating their dinner," and "don't make it a battle – you will never win," I changed my approach to meals and life became easier.

Ultimately we survived without them eating many vegetables, and even managed to travel throughout Europe and all over the world without them starving!

"Hello, I am a toddler and I love strawberry jam, strawberry ice-cream and pretty much everything strawberry except actual strawberries. Those taste terrible!"

# HARD TO SWALLOW (TRACEY)

The sun was shining and life was good. With great excitement my husband and I headed off to Philip Island on our first "solo" trip since our girls, Kathleen, 5, and Millie, 3, had been born. The girls were having a special sleepover at my parents, known to them as Nana and Pa. All were having a wonderful time until Pa decided to fix his computer whilst his small audience (Millie) watched on with great interest. She sat engrossed as he took the tiny screws out one by one- noting her fascination, Pa carefully warned her not to touch them and left the room to get a small jar to put them in for safekeeping.

What he forgot was the given rule that whenever you tell a 3 year old not to do something, they immediately do it! I can only imagine his horror upon returning, when not a single screw was to be seen. Visions of the next day's headlines swam before his eyes….

"Grandpa screws up!"

"Grandpa with loose screws!"

With trepidation, and already knowing the answer, he asked Millie where the screws were...

Meekly she gave her reply, "I ate them, Pa."

Minutes later I received a call from my very upset and contrite Dad (thank goodness for mobile phones- although at times ignorance would be bliss!) informing me of what had transpired. After determining that Millie was perfectly happy and showing no signs of distress, we decided to risk it and stay away. (I must say I slept with the phone next to my ear!)

Needless to say Millie survived and we spent the next few days playing search through the dirty nappy for tiny screws – not a particularly fun game! We were very relieved when they finally worked their way through her system.

This is not the way I recommend getting iron supplements into your child, nor was it conducive to further babysitting offers!

"How can you really know something if you haven't put it in your mouth?"

# HUMPTY DUMPTY (TRACEY)

When the girls were still young, we moved into our newly built two storey house. There were twelve steep steps that led up to the top floor, so we decided to lay carpet at the foot of the staircase in case any of them (or me) took a tumble. My husband and I were very conscious of them using the stairs, constantly admonishing them to be careful. When Louise was 2 going on 3, she was quite proficient at climbing, both up and down, but one particular day she somehow missed a step halfway down and somersaulted to the bottom! She landed on the carpeted area, but unfortunately rolled on to the tiles, banging her head quite hard. We heard the thump of her falling followed by the crack of her head on the tiles, then for a dreadful moment there was silence. Moments later the wailing began.

A large egg was forming on her head and we decided to take no chances, rushing to the emergency department at a nearby hospital. There they checked her thoroughly, including X-rays, and finally she was given the all clear. I thought the bump was going to last forever but gradually it subsided without a mark. There may have been no mark on her head, but our minds were certainly scarred.

From that day forth, and for a very long time, we were on "high stair alert" and I can never hear Humpty Dumpty recited without thinking of our little girl tumbling down our stairs!

How to fall down the stairs...

Step 1, Step 2, Step 4, Step 7...

# NIGHT TERRORS (LIS)

Night terrors are apparently relatively rare, occurring in only 3-6% of kids (mainly boys), and we won the jackpot, with both our boys experiencing them – at different times! As parents, it was the worst experience, being helpless to comfort them. I clearly remember sitting on our stairs waiting for the episode to pass. They shied away from being touched, and all we could do was wait it out. Thankfully this phase passed after a few months, never to return. They still suffered the occasional nightmare, but the hardest thing about those was only the return to an interrupted night's sleep; unlike the dreaded night terrors, a nightmare could be banished with a "mummy cuddle!"

Once they had started school one of our boys went through a phase of fearing someone would break into our house, so together we performed a nightly ritual of checking all the doors were locked to put his mind at ease. I could not believe my ears the day he came home from school asking me about Eloise Worledge, who had been kidnapped many years ago, taken from the safety of her bedroom while her parents slept a short distance away. This case had shaken

Melbourne families to the core, rocking parent's faith in their ability to keep their children safe, and a teacher's aide had decided, in her wisdom, to tell my six year old son about it! Whilst her intention may have been good, (apparently her son had suffered similar fears and had got over them) - what planet was she living on?! Now I had a little boy who was scared of people coming in through the window to take him!

We live in a two storey house, and although we had an intercom between the bedrooms, I guess Mum and Dad seemed another world away when his imagination went into overdrive. This led to our first major "twin" dilemma; he wanted a night light but his brother wanted complete darkness to sleep. This was not an easy problem to solve either because he didn't want his brother moving to another room! Many nights he would appear next to our bed having navigated the stairs in darkness, and I confess we succumbed to bad parenting and took the easy option of letting him crawl in with us. Of course, it had to be the one that wriggled and kicked in his sleep, not the one who never moved! Eventually he grew out of his fears, but to this day I still curse the lack of sense demonstrated by that teacher's aide and wonder how many kids ended up needing therapy after her "help!"

"Rock-a-bye baby, in the treetop

When the wind blows, the cradle will rock

When the bough breaks, the cradle will fall

And down will come baby, cradle and all!

And you seriously expect me to go to sleep now?"

# NIGHT OWL (TRACEY)

With three children, the odds are one of them is bound to keep you up at night. From the day she was born, Kathleen refused to go to sleep without a fight. She suffered from indigestion when breastfeeding, struggling to burp afterward, which left her extremely discontented. Every time we lay her in the bassinet to sleep, the howling would begin and continue until we picked her up. Once upright again, she would immediately settle. We tried everything from rocking her in a swinging pouch to the controlled crying technique; all to no avail. It seemed she needed very little sleep. (If only that was the case for us!)

18 months later, along came Millie, who had no problems sleeping, followed by Louise who I am glad followed in Millie's footsteps, not Kathleen's! Kathleen was a night owl from toddler to teenager, and even today (at 21) stays up very late.

On our family trip to the UK, we arrived at our hotel completely shattered from jet lag and crashed into bed. Kathleen (then 12) rose in the middle of the night; left the room, entered the lift, and descended to the lobby! Luckily, the security man, on duty at the reception desk, quickly realised she was in fact sleepwalking when she failed to respond to his questions. Gradually she came around and managed to tell him her name, enabling him to look up our room number and ring us. Unfortunately we were all dead to the world and failed to answer. The kind man then brought her up to the room and banged loudly until we finally answered. Imagine our shock when we opened the door to see Kathleen standing there! We were horrified to hear she had been sleepwalking and from that day forward blocked the door with a chair, hoping the commotion would wake us if she did it again.

I guess, like everything, there are exceptions to the rule and some kids just don't need their full eight hours. I know Kathleen certainly didn't!

"I don't like morning people...

Or mornings...

Or people!"

# LOCKED OUT (TRACEY)

It started as an ordinary day, me doing the household chores with Kathleen, 12 months old, busy mastering her first steps beside me. The washing was ready to hang out and I decided to leave Kathleen safely inside playing with her toys, whilst I pegged it on the line under the pergola, just a few steps away. It was a glorious day; the sun was shining, birds were chirping and Kathleen and I were loudly singing the Wiggle's classic, "Hot Potato," enjoying ourselves immensely.

How quickly things change; I heard a loud bang and spun quickly to see the back door had slammed shut, locking in the process! I gazed at the door in horror, having absolutely no idea what I was going to do. There was no spare key outside, and I was furious with myself for letting such a thing happen. There was no way my baby could open the door, and being 1995, there was no mobile to use to ring for help! Racking my brains for a solution, I called to Kathleen that I would be back shortly and raced to the neighbours, breaking all speed records to get there! I have never been so pleased to have someone answer my frantic knocking. Quickly I recounted what happened, and asked if I could use their phone to ring my husband. Although I'm sure they branded me "worst mum ever", they kindly allowed me in to their house. Thankfully my husband was working nearby, and he immediately left to come to our rescue. I hurried back home to reassure Kathleen that daddy would be there soon to open the door. She was nowhere to be seen through the windows.

Being unable to see your baby is totally unnerving and I immediately began fearing the worst. Minutes later (although it seemed a lifetime) daddy appeared to save the day!

The door opened to reveal Kathleen playing with her toys, quite unperturbed by all the fuss. I, on the other hand, was a shaking mess!

I learnt my lesson from that fateful day, and have always made sure there was a spare key hidden outside for such emergencies!

"Locked out of the house? I'll huff and I'll puff and I'll blow down the door!"

# IN THE GENES (LIS)

It's amazing how human beings are all so different and yet in some ways can be exactly the same. I have managed to pass on many of my traits to my kids and they have taken a fair few from Dad as well. There was much excitement when our boys entered the world and it was discovered that our first born had two toes on each foot joined together, just as I have. Webbed toes occur in approximately one in every 2,000 live births and whilst it is speculated to be an inherited condition, it is also common for only one family member to have them. Whatever the case may be, I have always claimed we are special, and having them has certainly not had any negative impact on our lives! Unfortunately Twin 1 seems to have inherited many of my medical problems, including sweaty hands and feet, headaches, and my infamous jaw line. Teeth were always going to be an issue for our kids with both my husband and I having crooked teeth (mine were corrected with orthodontics) and sure enough, both boys ended up wearing braces.

The orthodontist did a magnificent job with their teeth, but considerably less so in building body image, constantly telling one that he may require jaw surgery as he has his mum's apparently awful jaw line. I understand that he was looking for the perfect "dental face', but you'd think one would think twice before saying things to teenagers who are extremely vulnerable and sensitive to any implied fault they may have, warranted or not. It became our standing joke at each orthodontic visit; how long would it be before he mentioned jaw surgery? He never failed to deliver! While very grateful for straight teeth, we were all relieved when treatment finished and we no longer had to hear this.

Both boys when concentrating stick their tongues out, something I have done from a very young age; my dad's favourite photo of me shows my tongue in action while I pour from a teapot (taken at kindergarten). My brother in law created a photo montage of the boys and me, all with tongues out. Like mother, like sons!

One of my boys is double jointed as I am, although as I get older it is harder to get in the same positions I did in my youth! He managed for years to comfortably do the splits (and hold them) on a weekly basis at karate, much to the envy of his classmates. The other one has his dad's ability to eat everything in sight and not gain any weight, something I strongly resent; I only have to look at the food for weight to go on.

It is both special and bonding to share traits with family members, even problems; after all, a problem shared is a problem halved! I look forward to the day in the distant future when the boys have children and we see what features and characteristics they have passed on.

"That awkward moment when you find yourself frustrated with your child... for behaving just like you!"

# LIVING IN THE MOMENT (LIS)

The thing with parenting of babies and toddlers is that it takes over your whole world, and you can't remember, or imagine, a time when it wasn't like this. You are gob-smacked when you ask an older mum for advice on how to stop breast feeding and they don't remember! You think to yourself *'boy, I'll never forget something that important,'* but guess what – you do! You get annoyed at friends who call or visit at inopportune times, or plan something that doesn't fit in with your schedule of feeding and nap times! You think that these people are selfish and should know better, but trust me; the day will come when you too have crossed to the other side and I'm quite sure you will commit the very same crimes to the next generation of new parents. Try and be a little forgiving to us oldies who have been there and done that but are now in the next stage – we really don't mean to upset you!

My advice- if you can find the time- is to write everything down that could be handy. You never know who it could help!

"Mums are basically just part of a scientific experiment to prove that sleep is not a crucial part of human life."

# KIDS ON WHEELS (LIS)

An important milestone in every child's life is mastering the skill of riding a bike. Much fun has been had on scooters and tricycles, including a Fisher Price plastic tricycle that remains at our beach house to this very day, and which every kid that has ever been there loves and rides; I think the ridiculously overgrown eighteen year olds get more use out of it and enjoy it more than the toddlers ever did!

When the boys were older they progressed to real two wheeled bikes they received as birthday presents. I believe it was the learning of this skill that has led to many back problems, me running alongside trying to hold the back of the bike steady! One twin mastered it fairly quickly, whilst the other preferred to keep the safety net of the training wheels. One particular day he spent the morning trying in vain to get his balance without the trainers on, until finally in disgust he flung his bike on the grass and marched off into the house. Minutes later, he reappeared with a large piece of paper with *FOR*

*SALE* printed on it in big letters, and proceeded to stick it to his bike, waiting for potential customers to walk by! I still chuckle when I think of this, because the action sums up his personality perfectly; if he can't do something brilliantly, he won't do it at all, and he's always had a flair for the theatrical!

Happily I can say he did persevere and learnt to ride his bike with only two wheels. Many happy adventures were had with their Dad where they would set off for a ride, complete with drinks and snacks, and I would drive and pick them up from the designated destination.

At six we gave our boys a yellow electric ride-on car for Christmas (we had to compete with Santa somehow!) and they had many hours of fun driving up and down the street, taking it in turns at being driver and passenger. Here again their personalities stood out, one waving wildly to his audience and almost taking his brother's head off as he drove (this memory is etched in their Gramp's mind and he still often laughingly tells the story). And the other twin, eyes intently on the road, a perfect picture of concentration. Years later when they began driving, one persevered and now has a licence and car, and the other did not, happily choosing to take the bus instead- or, more likely, getting a lift from his 'chauffeur' brother! Just like his bike, he'll learn when *he's* ready, and only then.

My boys also had a motorbike which they rode up at Nanna's and Pa's home in the country. My husband and his three brothers had grown up riding motorbikes and this was something he wanted to share with his boys. (My learning to ride a motorbike ended with me crashing into the fence – nobody told me where the brake was!)

One of the hardest things about being a mum is losing your babies as they grow up: you wonder where the years have gone and look at the kids you have known since birth or kindergarten, and see them driving and drinking (not at the same time, obviously!) and somehow you can't quite grasp the fact that they are now an adult. It was the strangest feeling when I watched my son drive away alone from the dealers in his new car. To you, they will always be the little kids that you once knew; your precious babies will always be your babies, even when they are 50 years old!

"Let's go for a bike ride they said. It will be fun they said!"

# LITTLE FINGERS (TRACEY)

Mums have many things to worry about, but none more so than their children being hurt, and some suffer from a particular fear. Lis had a phobia about her boys injuring themselves with sticks (*"you'll take someone's eye out!"*), whilst my obsessive fear was little fingers being caught in cupboards or doors!

My nightmare became reality when Kathleen was about 5. We were away with friends at our holiday house, about to drive into town, when somehow- to this day I don't know how- her little fingers got caught in the car door as it slammed shut. I vividly remember her agonising screams and chalky white face. It was hard to get a look at her hand, as she didn't want to show us. Eventually we calmed her enough to examine them, but couldn't tell if they were broken, so off we set to the nearby hospital. The five minute drive was interminably long, with me cradling Kathleen in the backseat and reassuring her everything was going to be fine. I felt as bad as, if not worse, than she did; as a mum you desperately want to take the pain away, and if you could would gladly take it yourself.

At the hospital a kind nurse examined Kathleen's fingers and told her how lucky she was, and then gently wrapped them in a gauze bandage to keep them straight whilst they mended. The bandage was enormous, and Kathleen was extremely proud of her injury, showing it to everyone and milking it for all it was worth! From that day forward I never shut a door of any kind without checking to make sure all fingers were well clear, and even now although my girls are all old enough to look after their own fingers, I automatically check. Once slammed, twice shy!

"No matter how old our children are, when they hurt, we hurt...!"

# Naughty and Nice (Lis)

Kids have an uncanny ability to know exactly what to say and do to get out of trouble, and my boys were no exception to this rule (in fact, they excelled at it and still do). When sent to their rooms to think about what they had done wrong, a short time would elapse then they would appear, full of remorse. Big, wide eyes and "I'm sorry mummy, can I have a cuddle" never failed to win me over. My dad always said they knew exactly what buttons to push to get back in my good books, and he wasn't wrong. It's hard to resist an apology when it is gift wrapped with a big cuddle!

Then there was my all-time favourite apology; "It's ok mummy, I've put the naughty Daniel in the rubbish bin and shut the lid! The good Daniel is here now." I'm happy to say for the most part the naughty Daniel stayed put in the rubbish bin, but there's still the odd occasion when I wish the good Daniel would put him in the bin; the only problem is, these days we'd need a much bigger bin!

After reading the boys *Teddy Robinson*, a favourite book from my childhood about a cuddly but accident prone teddy bear, Callan adopted the expression "I'm fragile!" No more was he sad, tired or grumpy, instead he would state "I'm a bit fragile" in honour of Teddy Robinson! (This was unbearably cute and lasted for quite some time!)

Every family has their own catch phrases and 'kiddy sayings" and each one belongs in your own treasure chest of happy memories....

"When they are good, they are very, very good and when they are bad they are horrid!"

# ACTIVITIES (TRACEY)

When our youngest daughter started primary school, I went back to work four days a week, working 9am-5pm at a local community bank. This meant that our three girls needed to go into after school care for three days, being spoilt and picked up by their Nana on the other day I worked. Over the primary school years they fluctuated between enjoying and hating aftercare. The centre was situated on the grounds of their primary school, making it very handy and close to my work. The activities provided for the kids were fabulous; I remember many unusual ones that the girls undertook. One evening I arrived to find them having a lesson in professional cupcake making, using fondants for icing. The little cupcakes had a number of different coloured fondant icings on each and looked fantastic. They had many guest people attend; teaching soccer skills, tennis and even Zumba dancing lessons.

Our youngest daughter was lucky and made a friend there that has over the years become her best friend. Throughout the school years they also attended a few other activities done after school.

Kathleen did more than ten years of modern dance with a local studio, performing each year with them on stage. Millie took a year of karate lessons which she really enjoyed and was great for her fitness. All three girls joined our local netball club and to this day are still involved in playing. As they each approached the age of 15, they were keen to get a part-time job and earn their own money. The older two girls landed jobs at the local KFC outlet and stayed there for some years. Louise, our youngest, found herself a job at the local Bakers Delight and really enjoys working there. They have all learnt important qualities from these experiences; to be polite, punctual and able to work in a team environment.

Needless to say I am very proud of what they have achieved and look forward to seeing the next chapters in their lives unfold. I believe travelling the world is a high priority on all of their lists but I just hope that they are happy and healthy, whatever path they choose.

"To be in your children's memories tomorrow, you have to be in their lives today."

# ACTIVITIES (LIS)

Taking kids to after school activities can be time consuming and tiring for mums, and I know I certainly enjoyed the last week of school term when most activities had finished. I was fortunate that they didn't attend a multitude of activities, and I definitely counted my blessings that I had boys when I saw friends preparing for their girls' dance concerts, involving sewing of costumes, makeup and hair! (I have enough trouble doing my own, let alone having to do someone else's!) Both boys attended swimming lessons until they got to an older age and their teacher changed. The new teacher was all about technique, preparing for Squad (potentially the Olympics in her mind), insisted on them wearing speedos to improve times, and didn't know the meaning of the word fun. Both boys quickly lost interest and I didn't mind; all I had wanted them to achieve was being capable swimmers.

Next came soccer, and Kanga Cricket, but neither held their interest, and footy was never really on their radar. They both took up tennis in Grade 2, and whilst one opted out after a term (he was left handed and found it awkward), the other continued until Year 12. I myself love tennis and play competition weekly, so I was happy to take him and stay and watch. I also ended up working for his tennis coach for a time.

Summer nights at tennis lessons were great, but winter was challenging, with me opting to stay in the warmth of the car wrapped in a scarf and gloves, but still watching. When they were older, twin 2 chose to stay at home, and became the minder of Tuesday night's dinner, chile con carne, stirring the mince and cooking the rice. Consequently, it is his standard go to meal when he elects to cook!

Thursdays were family meat pie and chips night being Karate training night. This twin 1 also did from Grade 2 until Year 11, when study hours increased and he stopped, just shy of his black belt. Watching one and a half hours of karate training was very tiring for me, but doing it certainly made him extremely fit! I often chuckle at the memory of me being stupid and doing the exercises whilst sitting in a chair; I actually managed to pull a muscle, which whilst being very funny was actually quite painful. From that moment on I swore off karate, either sitting or standing still!

The next week saw the class on the floor on their backs raising their legs above their head and much to my amusement when the guy directly in front of my chair lifted his legs; there was a loud emission of wind! I swear I turned purple choking back laughter and I could never again look him in the eye or see that exercise performed without having a giggle.

"It's the little moments together that make the best memories forever!"

# A SHOPPER IS BORN (TRACEY)

One day my husband had taken Kathleen with him to the bakery to buy a loaf of bread. Once there, he decided that Kathleen, then aged 6, was old enough to gain some independence and confidence, so gave her money and sent her into the shop on her own with instructions to ask for a loaf of bread. Kathleen had been to the bakery many times before, and loved their food, particularly their iced finger buns, which we often bought for a treat. Her dad stayed in the car and watched his little girl timidly approach the counter and speak to the sales lady. Beaming with pride, he watched Kathleen skip happily back to the car, then noticed she had an extra bag. When he queried what it was, Kathleen cheerfully replied it was her iced finger bun! Her father could not believe that she had been brazen enough to buy it, but Kathleen had figured it was a perfect opportunity to get what she wanted; and so our shopper was born!

If I ever ask Kathleen to buy something for me now, I only give her enough money for my purchase!

"Just let me shop and no-one gets hurt!"

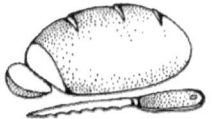

# COLLECTIONS (TRACEY)

Our girls certainly followed in their mother's footsteps when it came to collecting things. I have ever since I was a young girl, loved to collect things; Lis and I would spend hours scouring the beach for shells, our backs turning brown as berries from the hot sun. We had an enormous glass jar that we filled with 'pontoon shells,' small white shells with flat bottoms and a raised top, and these were used for betting money when we played cards. Just last year Lis returned to the beach we frequented and much to our delight after much searching found a pontoon shell.

The girls started out by collecting the toys which were found in each Happy Meal from McDonald's. These were usually a toy from the latest Disney or Pixar film, such as Toy Story or Monsters Inc. As they grew older they began collecting AFL Footy Cards which they kept in binders, each card having its own pocket in a plastic sleeve. Tazo discs were another favourite, and these were found in bags of potato chips. Strange how collectible items always came with chips or chocolate; never apples or carrots! I know it was not my finest parenting practice, but I would use these treats as rewards (or bribes!) to guarantee good behaviour. The Simpson's cards and discs were also a major hit- and according *influence-* with the girls.

It may not seem like an educational show, but I know my girls can thank The Simpsons for much of their knowledge of historical world events!

"It's amazing how much a few pieces of plastic and paper will sell for if the purchasers are parents or grandparents."

# RECOLLECTIONS AND COLLECTIONS (LIS)

Collections were very much a part of the boys' childhood, whether being books, stickers, magazines, cards or small plastic insects and animals. Harry Potter was very much a part of our world, and with each new movie release a sticker book was produced to go with it! Packets of stickers were purchased and then placed in the corresponding number in the book, or in our case two books, as each wanted their own copy. This had its advantages when dealing with doubled up stickers, but of course it ended up costing us twice as much! The show *Rugrats* also released a monthly series of magazines, each focussing on a different country. These were filled with interesting facts, and these, along with our travel, have largely contributed to the boys' extensive knowledge. (I did however put my foot down here, and only purchase one set!)

For a time Harry Potter chocolate frogs graced the supermarket shelves, and each of these came with a card. I do remember looking at our extensive pile of cards and wondering how it was the boys were not fat blobs with teeth falling out! Later, these chocolate treats were replaced with Kinder Surprises, a chocolate egg that held parts of a plastic animal or insect to be constructed. You might think these a waste of money, but they certainly had their use when the boys were in Primary School; many a project or diorama was decorated with said wildlife!

Back then, Golden Books could be purchased at the supermarket and every weekly shop I would add to our collection. These were cheap (as far as books go) and were perfect for a bedtime story. Golden Books were the very beginning of my kids' love affair with reading.

I must admit that I am very glad that they have well passed the stage of collecting; we all suffer from an inability to have a collection incomplete so it became an expensive hobby.

I envy those who can leave empty spaces in sticker books – that was never going to happen in our home. Now the boys can spend hours watching every episode of a TV show or fully completing a video game instead!

*"There is no app to replace your lap! Read to your kids!"*

# BAD TEACHER (TRACEY)

When Millie was in Grade 2, she started to become withdrawn and quiet. She asked me on several occasions if she could stay home, saying that she didn't feel very well. She didn't have a temperature and was happy enough playing with her sisters at home, but when it came time to go to school she would claim she felt unwell.

Eventually I sat down with her and asked her if everything was alright at school, or if anyone was being mean or nasty. She said she didn't like her teacher- "Mrs G." I asked her why and she told me in class she yelled all day. I offered to come and sit in class with her and see firsthand what was happening. She was very happy for me to do this.

The next morning I took Millie into her class with the other kids. I went up to Mrs G. and asked if I could sit at the back of the class and watch for a while. She said that was fine, so I grabbed a chair and sat out of the way, at the very back of the room. About 5 minutes later, Mrs. G actually started yelling at all the kids at the top of her voice.

*"NOW SIT DOWN EVERYONE! WILLIAM, IF YOU DON'T STOP DOING THAT I WILL SEND YOU TO THE PRINCIPAL, I HAVE TOLD YOU ALL A HUNDRED TIMES, LISTEN TO WHAT I AM SAYING! WHY DIDN'T YOU GO TO THE TOILET BEFORE MARY, QUIET EVERYONE, THAT'S ENOUGH WILLIAM, STOP PUSHING BEN, THOMAS!"*

After 10 minutes of continuous yelling, I understood why Millie wasn't enjoying school - neither was I! The teacher pulled out a book to read to the class, but before she began little Thomas yelled out to her "Mrs G, Ben said the 'F' word!" Ben looked mortified and yelled out "I never did Mrs G!" From where I was sitting, I was sure that Ben had not said anything and that Thomas was just trying to get Ben in trouble. Mrs G had no such doubts.

She yelled at Ben at the top of her voice: *"I WILL NOT STAND FOR THAT LANGUAGE IN MY CLASSROOM BENJAMIN, YOU ARE TO GO AND STAND OUTSIDE THE DOOR AND I WILL BE SENDING YOU TO THE PRINCIPAL!"* Ben tried again and with his voice quivering whimpered, "But I never said it Mrs G!" Again, she just yelled- *"YOUR BEHAVIOUR IS INTOLERABLE, I WILL NOT STAND FOR IT, OUT, NOW!"* Had Mrs G forgotten that I was sitting up the back watching all of this?

Ben began to cry and slowly made his way to the classroom door. I felt so sorry for him; my eyes began to well. Above all I was so sorry for Millie having to endure this for three quarters of the school year. I looked at Millie sitting quietly cross legged on the floor with the other kids. She was looking at the teacher, wide eyed with fear. It was awful. I'd seen enough, and excused myself and left the room. I went straight to the office and asked to see the Principal. After a short wait, sitting fuming, I met the Principal and aired my concerns and total dissatisfaction. How could Mrs G be allowed to teach like that? I told him under no circumstances would I allow Millie to be taught by her in the following years and if it occurred I would pull her from the school. The Principal told me I wasn't the first to complain and they would not be renewing her teaching contract at the end of the year. I was relieved to hear this but Millie still had 2 months of this awful teacher to endure!

I was so distressed; I really didn't want her to go through this any longer. At school pickup I spoke to other mums and learned they all felt the same way. That night we sat Millie down and told her that Mrs G would be leaving the school in 2 months, and could she try to stick it out; if she got too upset she was to go straight to the Office and ask the Principal to ring Mum. Luckily, that didn't happen and Millie survived the last 2 months of Grade 2.

I guess kids are often far more resilient than we realise and can put up with much more than we expect.

"Teach children WHAT to think and you limit them to your ideas. Teach children HOW to think and their ideas are unlimited."

# NESSIE (TRACEY)

When the girls were in their kindergarten years there were many shows on Nickelodeon to keep them entertained. One particular favourite was "Art Attack," in which the host showed you step by step how to create wonderful artwork. One project we fell in love with was making a Loch Ness Monster from flour and water, so off to our kitchen we went!

We mixed the ingredients, rolled the dough and then formed the two cylindrical shapes required. The girls had always loved making things with play dough or clay, and this was no exception!

The shapes were placed on each end of foil covered oven trays, thus creating an arch. These formed the body of Nessie, creating an illusion of her swimming with half her body submerged under water. Two more dough mixtures formed the head and tail and completed our swimming monster. Each Nessie baked in the oven for two hours. Impatiently the girls waited for them to cool so they could commence painting! Millie chose a metallic green and then decorated it with red circles.

We finished our brushwork and sat them in the sun to dry; the result was spectacular! This activity provided hours of fun, and taught the girls a different perspective when looking at objects. They loved the magical illusion and the way the brain and eyes can be tricked into thinking something exists that isn't really there (the body under the water).

To this day our swimming Nessies proudly guard our china cabinet alongside many other treasured mementos from special times…

"The perfect man is like the Loch Ness Monster… they say he exists but no one's ever seen him!"

# HIGH JINX (LIS)

Things change when your child goes out into the wide world without you; no longer are you the centre of their universe (for me, this was when they began 4 year old Kinder), and they became subject to other influences - not always good! So it was one day when a friend from kinder came around to play. He lived around the corner; however, I was amazed when he turned up at our door by himself. Admittedly, it was only a three minute walk from his home to ours, but I would certainly not have let mine do it alone! When they went on play dates I went too; we were a package deal!

My boys had the run of the house in which to play and they would quite often go upstairs on their own so I thought nothing of it when the three of them headed upstairs. Things however grew very quiet (and any mum knows that spells trouble!) so I went to investigate. Imagine my horror when I saw the three of them perched on the railing of our balcony that adjoins our bedroom – it's a four metre drop to the concrete below! Although inwardly I was petrified, I calmly told them to hop down and come inside, and then told their friend it was time to go home. Once he had left I sat my two down and asked them what on earth were they thinking climbing up there- didn't they know it was dangerous? They replied that it had been their friend's idea and they just went along with it....

Parenting lesson learned – things were changing in our world, and I needed to stay alert!

"If your friend jumped off a bridge, would you jump off a bridge too?"

# LITTLE MONKEY (TRACEY)

Our first born daughter, Kathleen, was a climber from the time she began to crawl. She would climb on anything within reach and it wasn't very long before she mastered climbing out of her cot! As a 2 and 3 year old, I would often find her guzzling milk, standing on the headrest of the couch, one hand clutching her bottle, the other clinging to the nearby curtain, looking exactly like a monkey perched in a tree. In our backyard was an open tree house, up to which she loved to climb. There she would sit for ages, solemnly gazing at the world below. Indoors too she didn't keep her feet on the ground, climbing the insides of doors, couches, tables – you name it, she climbed it.

When we moved house, much to Kathleen's (now aged 5) delight there was a tall, old fashioned street light right next to our driveway. Again the monkey in her emerged and she shimmied her way to the very top of the lamppost. Her younger sister of course immediately ran inside to tell us and when I saw her perched up there I was horrified. I demanded she climb down immediately (slowly and carefully), but the little minx was enjoying herself immensely. She knew I was powerless, so savoured the moment and took her sweet time before descending to join us!

"As a parent you realise you have a circus and untrained monkeys."

# MUMMY'S LITTLE HELPERS (LIS)

Be very careful what you say to your little ones; quite often they will take your words in the literal sense! I experienced this the day both of my boys were excitedly helping me put away the grocery shopping (boy, have those days long gone!). I passed one a twin pack of toilet rolls with clear instructions to put them in the downstairs toilet. …

Moments later I went to investigate, and yes, there they were; IN THE TOILET BOWL!

I suppose you can't say anything when they follow your instructions to a T, can you?

"Folding the washing with a toddler is like trying to straighten a desk full of papers while a fan blows on it."

# Computer Games (Tracey)

Our first ever PC was purchased in 1998, when Kathleen was four and Millie two (Louise was but a twinkle in her dad's eye). The girls loved playing games on the computer, including favourites such as '*Pyjama Sam,*' '*Thunder and lightning aren't so frightening,*' '*Freddy Fish*' and '*The Muppets Treasure Island*'. Often these games were mysteries where you had to solve clues and find hidden objects, using the mouse to click on the found item. Kathleen spent hours collecting objects, and then moving to the next level where she would begin anew. Millie, being younger, would happily 'colour in' using the mouse to select a colour, and then fill in an area of her chosen drawing, like a house or car. It was a simple and fun way for her to learn how to master using the mouse! As they grew older their game playing advanced just as technology did; PlayStation replaced PC, Nintendo DS's overtook Gameboys, iPods superceded the Walkman, and then came the iPhones… Favourite games that were repeatedly played were Spiro and Crash Bandicoot. My husband and

I were eternally thankful for Gameboys that were easily transported, making both car trips and holidays far less stressful, especially as they could play against one another. They loved problem solving, defeating bad guys and jumping and climbing their way through level after level. All three girls still love playing games, but these days it is mainly cards, chess or other board games, which are far more social! Computer games were certainly a major part of their childhood, and I believe they gave them great dexterity and motor skills which I know I certainly never developed from my time spent playing Space Invaders and Pacman back in the good old days!

"Computer games don't affect kids - if pacman had affected us as kids, we'd all be running around in a dark room munching magic pills and listening to repetitive music!"

# COMPUTER GAMES (LIS)

I have always loved technology, especially playing games, but my husband certainly does not! (For a time he did love playing Digger on the PC and Paganitzu, a puzzle game, but that was pre kids!) I loved the challenge of mastering the game, and have a strong competitive streak that does not let me give in! When the boys were old enough the gaming began, beginning with a chicken that laid eggs that you had to catch in a basket (helping them learn to count) on the old Sega. Then came the PlayStation, and it never left- although it did upgrade a few times along the way! We spent many an afternoon playing *Croc*, Spiro, Crash Bandicoot and various racing games. Most of these games had music or catchphrases that would echo in my head at night when I lay trying to sleep! Playing together was loads of fun, and my favourite memory is when we went to the haunted mansion in Disneyland, Paris and discovered it was just as it was portrayed in the game, bringing an old favourite game truly to life! Although technology games were extremely popular, we also loved playing board games and cards as well. One of the things I love most about our holiday house is the game playing! We do have a small

TV, but it generally only goes on for the news or a special sport event. We have the old SEGA machine down there, and I must say that for all the kids' prowess now with their PCs and PlayStations, I am still the queen of Teddy Boy! Other families often join us for weekends away and there is something special about sitting around the fire either chatting, reading or playing games. Much as I love technology, I treasure times spent with my family and friends and know I could certainly survive in a 'technology free world' (my husband would no doubt dispute this!).

"Wi-fi went down for five minutes so I had to talk to my family. They seem like nice people."

# A HAIRY TALE (LIS)

Haircuts have always been a drama in our house, and it is only recently that it has ceased to be a trauma. The boys' first hair cut was not a success, and involved many tears. I had not anticipated any trouble and was completely caught unawares at how upset they were. In retrospect, if I had known what was to come I would have approached the situation very differently.

I believe that one of the boys had a fear of scissors and loud noises and I know that they both hated the clippers (much as our dog does now!). I think that sometimes it is one of the few disadvantages about twins; they tend to feed off one another's fears!

I dreaded each visit and even did research to find 'kid friendly' hairdressers. I managed to find one, and although it was some distance from home, I figured it would be worth the drive. Unfortunately, however, the damage had been done. It was a brilliant set up; special kids size chairs, capes decorated with trains, teddy bears or princesses and a set of tools for the 'victim' to play with (including a spray bottle filled with water). But it was all too late. I think that if I had gone there for their first cut it would have been a different story, but alas, that was not the case and I was doomed to years of misery…

Most times we would make the trip on the weekend when my husband could provide an extra pair of hands and share the stress. Even with Nanna and Pa in tow, and the promise (bribe) of seeing Santa and getting a gift afterwards had no effect; haircuts were just a no go in our house! If I could cut hair at all I would have done it myself, however my one and only attempt at hairdressing ended with my husband sporting a "bowl" hairdo! (Not a good look!)

Unfortunately I think I must take the blame for this hatred of haircuts. Apparently when I was about 8, I ran out of the hairdressers whilst in the middle of getting my haircut. I had been sitting there with a scowl on my face when the hairdresser (I believe she was getting her revenge for my sour face) claimed she saw a nit egg. That was enough to make me take off! No, there were no nits, just an evil hairdresser and a scarred child who hated haircuts even more after that. So perhaps the hating of haircuts is "HAIREDITARY"!

As if the whole process was not bad enough, at age four it went further downhill. A photographer was due at Kinder the next week to do a shoot on each of the kids, meaning haircuts were in order. Off we set, but on this visit somehow the razor came out and a number one shave resulted. I was horrified when I realised, but it was too late; any intervention would only result in a stripe on their heads! Instead, their first 'school' photos had our boys looking like shaved convicts! I still cringe when I look at those pictures, and I don't think either of the boys has ever gotten their hair cut that short again. The one positive from this was it was quite a while before the next haircut was needed!

"Remember when you were young how tragic a simple haircut was!"

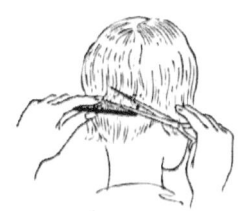

# FISHY BUSINESS (TRACEY)

When the girls were aged 10, 8, and 6, we were fortunate enough to have a large aquarium offered to us for free. Excitedly we all hopped in the car and set off to the pet store to get the necessary equipment (and of course fish). We had no idea that it was such an involved process; having to purchase a pump, filter, lights, stones and underwater features that would make it look fabulous. Of course these items did not come cheaply; the total was climbing and we hadn't even picked any fish yet!

We selected a mixture of small and bigger fish, and these were placed in a clear plastic bag to transport them home (I had visions of the scene with the fish tank in the dentist's room in *Finding Nemo*!) We also bought an enormous bag of fish food.

Once home we began the exciting process of filling the tank; we had been advised to acclimatise the fish slowly, so they didn't die of shock in freezing water! Soon everything was in place and looking fantastic; we all loved watching the fish swim. It's very relaxing (you often find them in doctors and psychologists rooms) and we figured it was a cheap therapy option!

Night time was particularly spectacular when we turned off all lights bar the tank light, and watched the fish darting around. Sometime later, my husband bought home a yabby from work and placed it in the tank. All went swimmingly (ha-ha) until one weekend we went away, only to return and find that the yabby had disappeared! The girls searched the tank thoroughly but he was nowhere to be seen. A few days later, we found him dead on the lounge room floor! Further investigation revealed that he had made his escape through the small lid on top of the tank. Obviously he had been searching for food, but unfortunately, there was none to be found.

The girls were very sad and concerned that the fish too may pass away. Happily the fish survived for many years and eventually we sold the tank (and fish) to a family with young children.

"If fish don't have hands, where do fish fingers come from?"

# FOUR LEGGED FRIENDS (LIS)

Pets have always been a part of our family, both before and after children. My husband brought me a dog as a wedding present, and that gorgeous girl Jessie shared our lives for a wonderful 17 years. Her only flaw was she was a Houdini, who loved to escape and go wandering. My husband and his mate Paul spent one afternoon "escape proofing" the gate. Finally they came in for a well-earned beer, very smug with themselves. "That'll fix her," they crowed, just as I glanced out the window, and saw Jessie happily trotting up the driveway! She used to come and meet me at the tram stop after work, and I could never decide whether to yell at her or hug her!

When she was 10 we decided to get another dog, and having a puppy around certainly gave her a new lease of life. When the boys were born we were given some good advice and took the blankets and clothes that they had used home and let the dogs sniff them. Consequently when we arrived home from hospital and placed the two capsules on the floor, both dogs had a quick sniff, and that was that! The boys loved those dogs as much as we did and although it was hard work manoeuvring a double pram and two dogs, somehow

I managed.

Sadly Jessie's time finally came and the boys (aged 3), Stu and I spent the morning cuddling her and saying goodbye. Many tears were shed; we didn't try to hide how upset we were, so neither did they. Afterwards we bought a rose and had a plaque engraved "*In memory of Jessie – Bestest dog in the world*" which still sits in our garden today.

Since then we have lost three dogs, each time harder as the boys were older and had a larger understanding of death. I found things to help them cope; we made photo albums of each dog, printed and framed the poem "The Rainbow Bridge," and placed it with a photo next to their bed.

Our dogs have provided our boys with much love and happiness and given them memories that will last a lifetime. They really are man's best friend.

"Dogs have a way of finding the people who need them and filling a space we didn't even know we had."

# THE RAINBOW BRIDGE

Just this side of heaven is a place called Rainbow Bridge.

When an animal dies that has been especially close to someone here, that pet goes to Rainbow Bridge. There are meadows and hills for all of our special friends so they can run and play together. There is plenty of food, water and sunshine, and our friends are warm and comfortable.

All the animals who had been ill and old are restored to health and vigour. Those who were hurt or maimed are made whole and strong again, just as we remember them in our dreams of days and times gone by. The animals are happy and content, except for one small thing; they each miss someone very special to them, who had to be left behind.

They all run and play together, but the day comes when one suddenly stops and looks into the distance. His bright eyes are intent. His eager body quivers. Suddenly he begins to run from the group, flying over the green grass, his legs carrying him faster and faster.

You have been spotted, and when you and your special friend finally meet, you cling together in joyous reunion, never to be parted again. The happy kisses rain upon your face; your hands again caress the beloved head, and you look once more into the trusting eyes of your pet, so long gone from your life but never absent from your heart.

Then you cross Rainbow Bridge together....

*Author Unknown.*

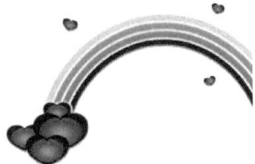

# SPECIAL FRIENDS (LIS)

My kids have had various soft toys over the years of which a chosen few became "extra special". Sleep would not be achieved without said special friend, and of course everywhere the kids went, they went. These included a knitted Noddy and Big Ears, a Scooby Doo dog from Movie World, a Panda that had been mine and a teddy which had also been mine, given when I was born. (Needless to say he was totally threadbare and had a sporadic squeak!)

I had never been a doll lover as a little girl; instead I had my family of stuffed animals, all of which had to sleep in bed with me. My kids followed in my footsteps, and given that they were boys, it was probably a good thing I never favoured dolls! Eventually Oscar Bear and Woofy Dog (AKA Woofster) became the boys' ultimate best friends and shared both their beds and secrets for many years.

I have fond memories of travelling through Europe with the boys (age 6) and Oscar's head poking out of Daniel's backpack. Oscar drew many smiles from fellow travellers, and I must say he behaved impeccably the whole trip! The same cannot be said for the panda that travelled to Vanuatu with us, who decided to have an adventure and check out the hotel's laundry service! He had become tangled in the bedsheets and eventually after some frantic searching by us, and with help from hotel staff, was safely located and returned to us by bedtime (saving much drama and tears!)

I'm sure all mums dread the loss of a special toy, or have some scheme to achieve getting them washed and dried between nap times without World War 3 occurring! I would constantly tell the boys to leave their "friends" in the car whilst we were shopping so they wouldn't get lost, but invariably I would give in, and off we would go, toys in tow! Inevitably one day disaster struck and Scooby was left behind in the book department at David Jones. His absence was not discovered until we arrived home, by which time the shops had closed! I had a sleepless night, with visions of having to return to Movie World for a replacement (yes, this was before the internet made life so much easier). Imagine my relief the following morning when I rang and was informed yes, indeed, Scooby was there! Off we set to collect him and on arrival found him under the counter, safely tucked in a bag with a jumper under his head for a pillow! I guess the sales lady who put him there was a mum; I know even now it tugs at my heart strings when I see a furry friend alone on a seat somewhere.

The only other loss was when we were at Playgroup (attached to a local church). One of the other kids had taken a shine to Woofy, and again after a major search party with no luck, we finally located him in the church, religiously sitting on a pew, praying for his little owner to come and find him!

Lesson finally learnt – special friends stay at home unless it's a holiday or a sleepover!

"There's a rip and a tear in my teddy bear... and love pours out from him everywhere!"

# ODD SOCKS (TRACEY)

The biggest problem with socks and babies is keeping them on! Every time I put a pair on the girls they would invariably work their way off to be found in the cot, pram, car, or on the shopping centre floor. Countless times I was stopped by people returning our stray socks with knowing smiles and an *"I think this may be yours."* When the girls were older we were often in a hurry, getting ready for Kinder, school and outings. I was never big on matching socks when folding the laundry; so as long as they were the right size, on they would go! The girls never seemed at all concerned that they didn't match. School was easy- white socks were easily matched- but weekends were a completely different matter. Having spent previous years wearing odd socks the girls would just grab any that were available, matching or not. People made many comments, and odd socks became somewhat of a Samios trademark! When they were teenagers I bought each of the girls their own sets of socks but still they managed to get mixed and became 'common property'. I had also bought different ones for myself but still the girls raided my sock drawer; it seems it is an unspoken agreement in our house that socks are fair game and belong to all! I'm glad that we are comfortable with wearing non matching socks; It shows me we are happy with ourselves and don't feel the need to conform to the norm! Just this morning I looked in my drawer to see I had a choice of a matching pair or odd socks. Purposely I picked two of different colours and put them on. I wonder if the girls do the same…

"What if the dryer has been stealing all our clothes, but for years we have only noticed the socks because they come in pairs?"

# SOCK HORROR (LIS)

How can innocuous objects such as socks create so much grief in so many homes? It is a common complaint of mums worldwide that washing machines eat socks, and I am a definite believer! Our laundry has a container filled with odd socks just waiting for their missing partner to miraculously appear. Sometimes this actually does occur, usually at the next wash, when an errant child has found it under their bed or tucked in the leg of jeans. Occasionally they would be tangled in my ironing pile and were discovered when I did the ironing, but more often than not they disappear, never to be seen again. However, I am very reluctant to throw any odd sock out, as I know that as soon as I do its partner will magically appear!

I do remember on a couple of occasions having to remove unwashed school socks from the washing machine as the kids had run out! At $8 a pair, we had minimum supply and all it took was a slack washerwoman to create a disaster. The school had strict uniform regulations and detentions could be given for violations. Neither of my boys had ever received detentions and I am happy to say they (like me) completed their school days without ever getting one. The same, however, cannot be said for their father! Wearing unwashed socks on the odd occasion was okay, but it was a traumatic day when it was found there were none clean and the washing machine had just started. In vain I tried to dry them in the dryer, but we had no time! Luckily it was winter time, so a black pair was worn. It would have been diabolical if it had been summer; you can't hide wearing black socks with shorts!

Every mum has their pet hates, and one of my biggest was socks being put in the wash inside out. It made sorting the clean washing that much harder (and more time consuming) when I had to turn them in the right way before rolling them into pairs. Repeatedly I asked the boys to please put them in **not** inside out, but to no avail. Finally, in exasperation I created a rule; for each sock that was inside out $1 would be deducted from their weekly pocket money!

Magically all socks suddenly came out the right way! Such a small thing, but I was in heaven; I should have created that rule years before!

"Nothing is really lost until your Mum can't find it!"

# BIRTHDAYS (LIS)

Birthdays are, and always were, a big deal in our house. Parties and celebrations occur every year and when the boys were little I would spend the weeks, with a few sleepless nights, leading up to their birthday planning the perfect party and presents. Each year became a new challenge to come up with something different – no McDonald's or Rollerama parties for us! I wanted something special and unique that the kids would love and always remember. My girlfriends began to refer to me as The Party Queen, a title I was, and still am, proud of. The stress and worry faded to nothing the instant I saw their shining faces as they unwrapped their presents or enjoyed their parties. They were certainly spoiled but I figured they were worth it, and we only had to do one big birthday each year! The memories of their birthdays are ones I will cherish forever.

We began with a relatively normal jumping castle, progressed to a fire engine (which took the kids for a ride around the block), a Harry Potter Puppet show, a clown, a Mad Scientist party (complete with Segway rides), a trip to the Circus, a day at Gumbuya Park (a fun park), and at Little Devils Circus, where they got to perform acrobats and circus tricks for the day.

Two of my (and their) all-time favourites were the ones that I created myself; "The Mystery of the Pilfered Pooch," and "Medieval Mayhem," mystery parties where the kids dressed in character, acted out a script and solved the mystery, much like the murder mystery parties of old (with no violence).

Add themed games to the mix - archery, jousting, bobbing for apples and a medieval feast and it was a perfect party. EBay and op shops are perfect places to shop for props and costumes and this all adds to the fun.

These parties are what eventually led to the forming of our Etsy shop, KidsMysteryGames, where a variety of themed parties for both boys and girls can be purchased.

(You can view it here- www.etsy.kidsmysterygames.com.)

One of my boys actually wrote *Medieval Mystery and Mayhem*, so it may not surprise you to learn he is now studying Journalism (and Law) at University! Tracey and I created the Etsy shop with me writing the majority of stories (another girlfriend penned several) and Tracey designing the invitations, other graphics and being a marketing marvel! I still get the same thrill when I hear the *chaching* sound on my iPad signifying a sale as I did with the first!

Tracey and I also run another Etsy store, *"Little Owls and Pals"* where we sell knitted animals and fabric dolls and animals that we have made ourselves. I love that we share so much together and it has certainly enhanced our already awesome friendship.

"My daughter wanted a Cinderella themed party so I invited all her friends and made them clean the house!"

# MOTHER'S WORRY (TRACEY)

I have always been overprotective and a worry wart of a mother. I don't think I'm overboard about it; I just see it as caring about my children. During the primary school years there were countless daily bus excursions that took the girls out with their teachers all over the place to broaden their knowledge about the outside world. Usually once a year there was a 3 day camp somewhere, which I privately dreaded, spending the whole time worrying about them. The girls always had a ball, and thankfully nothing bad ever happened, despite all my stressing. After they returned home from a camp I would see the photos of the daring flying fox rides, huge drop-swings and high off the ground suspended rope challenges. In a way, I was glad I found out about these events *after* they happened!

I struggled each year when the girls had their swimming lessons. I would even try to attend when I could to be an extra set of eyes on the sidelines. Don't get me wrong, I was all for them learning to swim- it's a fabulous programme that the school do- but I would really worry that the girls could be struggling in the pool and may be missed by the swimming instructors who had to try and keep an eye on a dozen students all at once. I had experienced a moment with Kathleen when she was 6, watching her struggle in a public pool, and it was hard to let go of the memory and worry from that time. But once again, all was fine, and the girls learnt how to swim without incident. As the years rolled on, carnival and show rides became a big draw for the girls, just as they had in my teenager years, but I always worried when they hopped on a mechanical ride at the local fete, Luna Park or the Royal Melbourne Show. I was always wondering, *have they been maintained well by the operators? Are they strapped in tightly enough?* Of course, they were, but you just can't let the worry go sometimes.

In secondary school there was a subject they all decided to take called "*Pushing the Boundaries.*" (It certainly pushed my boundaries!) Just as it sounds, it involved the girls partaking in events that they would find challenging. I remember some included learning how to surf, underwater diving (much to my relief they decided not to partake in this one) kayaking and abseiling to name but a few. I have tried not to stop the girls trying things and have gotten better over the years, but when they sign up for something which basically puts them in potentially dangerous situations, I cannot stop myself getting stressed and have had to learn to overcome my fears.

Another worry has been teaching 3 daughters to drive, each requiring 120 hours of experience before sitting their licence test. And when they pass, watching them drive off alone is a surreal feeling; both helpless and proud! Our most recent worry has been our second daughter travelling over to Europe on a Uni exchange. At 19, it is her first solo trip without the family and I'm happy to say that she is coping extremely well. We are so very proud of all of our daughters and, although I still worry about them, they have grown to be very capable, extraordinary young women.

"I always worry about the safety of my children... especially the daughter that is talking back to me now."

# MUMMY POLITICS (LIS)

Arguably, one of the hardest things about your kids starting school is the fact that you end up back in the schoolyard yourself. There you will be judged on your children, parenting skills, dress sense, and even the car that you drive! If you thought that your days of cliques and bitchiness were behind you, think again ; school mums come in all shapes and sizes, just as your teenage peers did, and be warned, there are plenty of mean ones as well as nice.

I was very involved with the boys' schools and loved helping when and wherever I could. That was my choice, and one that I have never regretted but I did receive plenty of snide remarks along the way, generally from working mums commenting on how nice it must be to have so much free time. It had been our choice for me to be a "stay home mum", and whilst I resented being judged, I am lucky enough to have enough self-esteem not to care too much about the bitchier mums and their comments. I made several true friends that shared the school journey with me, and most remain friends today.

"Mummy Politics" should be avoided at all costs. Follow the mantra of the Penguins of Madagascar; "Just smile and wave, girls. Smile and wave…"

You will soon find your own kind that you can relate to and funnily enough generally you will find these are the parents of the kids yours have made friends with, proving that the apple generally doesn't fall far from the tree!

Your kids too will usually find themselves victims of schoolyard politics at some point in their school life, and mine were no exception. They had both decided to nominate for School Captain of their Primary School and had, after giving speeches, both been voted into the last three. That was when the war began, and just like real politics, it grew ugly and had one candidate making false promises (a pool for the schoolyard)! Happily one of my boys was elected School Captain and the other Environment Captain, making me a very proud Mamma Bear! However, it had been a torrid week and certainly deterred my boys from applying for future leadership roles.

It did teach them valuable life lessons; not everyone plays fair, and not everyone can be a winner. But this time, they both were.

"Just smile and wave girls, smile and wave...."

# NINE ELEVEN (TRACEY)

Once Kathleen started primary school, we got out of the habit of turning the television on in the morning. It was proving to be too much of a distraction whilst she was getting ready. And yet, on the morning of September 11th 2001, for some unknown reason, I turned it on. I was in total shock at the images I saw. The girls all asked what was happening and I struggled with what to tell them. Eventually I pulled myself together and took Kathleen to school, the younger ones in tow. Once back home, I sat and watched the coverage all day; Millie and Louise were too young to understand what was happening, but they knew from my mood something was very wrong. It was one of those moments where you remember every detail; where you were, what time it was and what you were doing. So it was when Princess Diana died; I was shopping and the lady on the door at Target gave me the sad news.

"I wouldn't change my children for the world, but I wish I could change the world for my children."

# PLAYING NOT POLISHING (LIS)

One of my favourite things about being a mum was playing with my boys- maybe it's because I'm just a big kid at heart! I loved taking them to the park for picnics and spent many a summer afternoon in the sandpit that my husband had transformed from an old fernery. We created cities, built roads with their digger, and dug moats which were then filled with water. I loved making things, and following suggestions from shows such as Playschool, made them everything from rattles (old soft drink bottles filled with rice) to brown paper bag puppets. We made our own play-dough and made papier-mâché piggy banks using balloons, newspaper, flour and water; I hasten to add they also had a toy box filled to the brim with store bought toys! They had a blackboard and chalk, and an easel for creating masterpieces (we had a friend who was a butcher and gave us reams of white paper) which made perfect, cheap, made-with-love wrapping paper for presents!

Finger painting or painting with potatoes (peeled with shapes cut out) was another favourite pastime, and even though many of these activities created a huge mess, the enjoyment we all had made it worthwhile. I like to think that in years to come they will look back and remember their mum playing and having fun with them, not stressing over whether the house was spotless, or yelling at them for making a mess. Memories are made with fun and laughter- not vacuums and dusters!

"Yesterday I cleaned my house which was dumb because I still have kids living here!"

# ROAD TRIP (TRACEY)

Our holiday home is situated in East Gippsland, about a three hour drive from our house. The usual route to get there passes through rolling green hills, small country towns, forests of gumtrees, a wind farm, and offers occasional glimpses of the sea. Although a picturesque drive, like anything that has been done countless times, it has become quite boring.

So it was that one trip when the girls were ages 9, 7, and 5, we decided to take an alternative route. We set off in the early afternoon, full of excitement and a sense of adventure and after driving for about an hour, decided on a whim to turn off the main highway onto a smaller road that we thought would prove to be a shortcut.

For a while all was well; the road was made, and the views were new. The kids were happily naming the animals they could see in the paddocks; sheep, cows, goats and horses. Ray and I decided to add to the fun and asked if they could see the giraffe! "Where, Where?" they all yelled, beside themselves with excitement. Then they caught on we were teasing and joined the fun, asking if we could see the elephant! This continued for some time, creating much laughter; we calmed only when we saw an echidna followed shortly by a blue tongue lizard. This was truly an "in the wild" trip and to add to the mix there was not a soul to be seen, nor had we passed any cars. We stopped to inspect the lizard, and then continued only to see a snake slither across our path; we voted to pass on taking a closer look at him!

The sun was sinking low on the horizon and the road was no longer bitumen, but rather more of a lane flanked with densely overgrown foliage. We considered turning back but we'd come so far; surely our destination was close!

On and on we drove, seeing nothing until eventually we passed a wombat plodding slowly home. Darkness fell and the age old litany of kids in the car began; *"Are we there yet? I'm tired! I'm hungry!"*

A broken record, over and over; the fun adventure had turned to a nightmare!

Finally after an interminably long drive on our 'shortcut' we came to an intersection and nearly cried with joy. At last -we knew where we were! Together Ray and I breathed a huge sigh of relief, outwardly pretending we had always known exactly where we were!

Needless to say, there were no more shortcuts for us!

"Take a short cut they said... we'll get there faster they said...!"

# THAT'S WHERE CLOUDS COME FROM (TRACEY)

One day we were driving past the Loy Yang Power Station near Traralgon with Kathleen only 4 at the time, sitting in the back of the car. She gazed in awe at its size, totally entranced as we passed by; it looked like something from both the future and the past all rolled into one giant sci-fi building. Plumes of smoke spiralled from the four huge chimneys into the clear blue sky. Suddenly a look of realisation dawned on Kathleen's face and loudly, in a true eureka moment, she proclaimed *"THAT'S where the clouds come from!"*

"Some people are like clouds. Once they are gone, it's a beautiful day!"

# SO MUCH MORE THAN JUST A MUM (LIS)

A mum has so many roles to fill, some of the hardest being Santa, the Tooth Fairy, and the Easter Bunny. The pressure to fulfil those Santa lists, make sure money is placed under pillows, and hide those eggs gets harder each year as they get that little bit smarter! One of my biggest fears was that my boys would appear from their bedroom as I came down the stairs with their stockings filled to burst, ready to hang! Luckily this never occurred, and the closest we came to a disaster was the time the boys, whilst playing, found the Green Goblin glider toy that I had hidden, intending it to be a gift from Santa. Some quick thinking on my part and it became a present from Gramps that I had bought (they knew I did Gramp's shopping so this was plausible!)

The only other close shave was the time I woke at 4am and realised the Tooth Fairy had not done her duty; mad panic followed trying to find some money. I only had a $50 note in my purse and the Tooth Fairy sure wasn't feeling that generous! Eventually I located some coins in the car, and feeling very relieved, stealthily slipped them beneath the pillow.

I loved getting them what they wanted (yes, they were spoilt) and they generally got everything on their list. One does remind me jokingly he didn't get the life size remote controlled R2-D2 he wanted – with a price tag of just under $1000, I know that's hard to believe! I well remember the year they had just turned three and after asking for one thing for weeks, one decided the day before Christmas (three year olds are notorious for changing their minds!) all he REALLY wanted was a fire truck. One last minute mad dash to the shops and Santa came through again! (We still have the fire truck down at the beach house – a lasting memento of Santa's prowess!)

I remember the time I told the boys I wasn't sure where it was even possible to buy the requested present and got the confident response; "It's okay Mum, don't worry – Santa will bring it for me instead."

Aaaaaaggggghhhhhh!

Christmas is a special time in our house and each year our house is decorated with lights, the display growing as the boys get older and are able to put them up themselves; fairy lights, Santa and reindeer all have been added over the years. It is hard work to create but well worth the effort when they are finally switched on. Every night we would piggy back the boys outside (no wonder I have back problems now) and gaze in admiration at the scene before us. We would also do a drive around the area to check other people's lights and it definitely added to our festive spirit. When we took them to see *Elf* at the movies, tears sprung to my eyes seeing their wide eyed rapture as they watched the sleigh shoot through the sky. It was as if they were really witnessing magic on the screen; I still can't watch that scene without getting shivers!

Having kids around certainly puts the magic back into Christmas, and I think I loved it even more as a mum than I did as a child myself. We followed all the usual traditions, putting out beer and cookies for Santa and one year I added reindeer hair (cut from our dog Jessie's fur) for the boys to find. I will never forget the wonder on their faces when they found it.

Even when they were six weeks old (their first Christmas) I brought presents and wrapped them to put under the tree. Probably a good thing they couldn't unwrap them because when I opened one of the security blankets I had bought (one red Elmo and one blue Grover) a massive huntsman spider stared up at me! Some security blanket that turned out to be…

Sadly now the kids are young adults themselves and Christmas does not have the same sense of magic, no matter how hard we try. It's a special time when the lights and tree are put up and *Elf* is viewed - but that little bit of extra magic is sadly missing.

I hope that if and when the grandchildren come, the magic will return and I look forward to my kids playing Santa themselves. Anyone who says you shouldn't lie about the existence of Santa has obviously never felt the magic themselves. In this crazy, often scary world we live in, a little bit of magic, real or not, goes a long way.

"A Mum can replace many things but nothing and nobody can replace a Mum!"

# BLOW, BLOW, BLOW YOUR NOSE (LIS)

One unexpected challenge of being a parent was teaching the kids how to blow their nose! It never occurred to me this was something that had to be taught- I thought it was a natural instinctive behaviour, but it seemed this wasn't the case. Apparently only baby elephants are born thinking it makes sense to blow through your nose!

It is not an easy thing to teach and after much failure I turned to games to make it a fun exercise rather than a chore. We practiced blowing bubbles with bubble mix and a wand, in order to teach them how to breathe through their mouth. What kid doesn't love blowing bubbles? Once this was accomplished we moved on to another game, "Blow the Tissue." This involved the boys taking a big breath, clamping their teeth together, and trying to blow air from their nose on to a tissue that I held about an inch from their face. If the tissue moved I would yell "winner" and clap and cheer. Like every skill you need to master, it took lots of practice, but at least practice was fun – especially blowing out candles on birthday cakes!

Another surprise was their inability to swallow pills. Luckily drug companies kindly make most common kids' medications in liquid or chewable versions, but the day will inevitably come when you are prescribed something for your children that is only produced in tablet form; and this is not the time that you want to begin teaching them how to swallow pills! I discovered that placing the offending tablet in a spoonful of yogurt or ice cream was the key to success; the unwanted intruder slid down the throat without being felt. This proved a very handy tool when later I had to give the dog pills; I merely substituted butter for the yoghurt and down it would go!

Next came Growing Pains; something that I actually thought was an old wives tale! Imagine my surprise (and horror) when I discovered that they are an actual condition. Strangely, these pains can come and go, and will affect some kids more than others. One of my boys complained of pains, whilst the other never did! I read up on it (thank goodness for Google) and learned the best way for us to deal with them was with plenty of cuddles, massage and heat. (Either a bath or a heat pack did the trick)

I am sitting with a heat pack on my neck as I write this now; it seems I am suffering them too - GROWING OLD PAINS!

""I like sneezing, it's like blowing your nose, only your body does the work for you!"

# DOUBLE DOUBLE THIS THIS! (TRACEY)

There are many games and rhymes that your children will learn in the school playground, and many, surprisingly enough, are the same ones that we played in our childhood. I'm sure everyone remembers how the person who was to become "it" in tiggy or chasey would be chosen with the use of *eeny meeny miny moe* (I might add that in our day the version was politically incorrect with the line being '*catch a nigger by the toe*' – they were just words to us then but I look back in horror now!)

Hand clapping was a favourite game for the girls and this was accompanied by various songs; *Miss Mary Mack Mack Mack, All dressed in black, black black…under the bamboo tree, a sailor went to sea, to see what he could see!*

My favourite, and by far the most difficult game, involves knuckles/ hand tapping and my youngest daughter Louise and I still play it today! It requires quick thinking, fast actions and much skill, tapping each other's knuckles and the sides of your fists in unison whilst you chant the words; Double Double This This, Double Double That That, Double This, Double That, Double Double This That!

I seemed to always be the one to muck it up, others erupting in laughter as I begged "Do it again, do it again, I'll get it right this time!" I love that is a game that Louise and I have shared over the years and I hope we continue to play for many more! Perhaps it will help prevent my brain from turning to dust…

"I used to have functioning brain cells, but I traded them in for children."

# MUM KNOWS BEST (TRACEY)

Long car trips with kids aged 7, 5, and 3 can be a nightmare, as any mum would know! We generally headed to our humble holiday home (dubbed "The Shack") every couple of months, and with it came the three hour drive. We still do this, but nowadays usually only the youngest is still happy to accompany us for a whole weekend away.

In their younger years we played many games in the car with the girls to help pass the time; *I Spy,* 20 Questions, Spot the Yellow Car, and so on. Invariably, though, boredom would set in and the whinging would begin, increasing by the minute until it reached a crescendo; *"She touched me, she looked at me, she's looking out of MY window!"* – A Chinese water torture! This really soured what otherwise was a fabulous family time away from home.

One day whilst shopping I came across a portable DVD player, brand new on the market. *Eureka,* I thought- the perfect thing to guarantee peace in the car! The retail price of $450 was a stumbling block; my husband considered it totally unnecessary and a complete extravagance when I raised the idea. I remained undaunted. After many years of marriage I knew just what buttons to push and how to play it so I would get my way!

I bought the DVD player and sure enough Ray was initially disgusted. His tune soon changed, however, after a blissfully peaceful trip with the three girls glued to their favourite Disney film and he conceded that it had indeed been a brilliant idea (he should never have doubted me!)

Of course, being the gracious wife that I am, each time we arrived at The Shack I never failed to turn to him and sweetly say "I'm so glad I bought that DVD player."

"You don't know something? Google it.

You don't know someone? Facebook them.

You can't find something? Mum!"

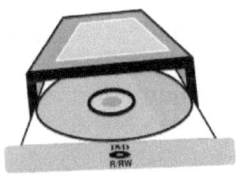

# NEVER ENDING EGGS (LIS)

Easter, like Christmas and birthdays, was a big event in our house, and the Easter Bunny's visit is very much anticipated. Chocolate is eaten for breakfast and the hunt for eggs is loads of fun! One particular Easter, Tracey and her family had come to our beach house with us and the five kids were having a wonderful time searching for eggs, then placing them in a large basket, ready to be divided equally at the finish. Kids were running everywhere, screaming delightedly each time they found one, whilst us four parents watched on. Then one of us had the bright idea of taking an egg from the "found" pile and hiding it again while the kids weren't looking! This worked a treat, so then the four of us took it in turns!

This went on for quite some time, us parents in hysterics and the kids beside themselves with excitement at how many eggs they were finding! Finally they caught on when they realised the total of eggs in the basket didn't seem to be increasing. (Note to parents: this will only work if you have a large number of eggs!)

Once they had started demolishing chocolate eggs we were all forgiven, and for Tracey and me, the memory of that particular Easter Hunt will last for forever.

"EASTER EGG HUNT IS ON...
EGGCELLENT! "

# MUM LOSES HER TEMPER (TRACEY)

I remember several times when my girls were growing up warning myself not to go overboard and lose my cool with them when I was angry. I had read several parenting books and knew that my girls were really quite good, but the one thing that I just couldn't abide was them being mean to each other, especially when they ganged up two on one; this would really upset me and cause my blood to boil! Luckily, they only ever used their words to hurt. I had taught them from a very young age to never, *ever* physically hurt each other. A typical argument would begin with the two eldest giving the youngest a hard time, telling her *"you can't have a turn, you're too small,"* and so on. The youngest would beg and try her hardest to be included but they would constantly refuse. Things would escalate fairly quickly, like putting a match to paper, and soon all three would be screaming from *"it's not fair!"* to *"it's my turn!"* to their favourite battle cry - *"MAKE HER DO THIS, MUM!"* Eventually after listening to this for a while, I finally snapped and yelled; *"LOOK, you three, I've had it up to HERE!"* and gestured with my hand to the top of my head

- boiling point! For some strange reason this caused all three to stop and stare, then erupt in uncontrollable laughter. My eldest said, "So mum, you've had it up to *here* have you?" She then placed her hand above her head like mine. "Any more and you'll explode!" This caused further hysteria, and I must say it is hard to remain angry in the face of such mirth. I figured if you can't beat them, join them and I too burst into laughter. To this day, whenever I start to get annoyed they will remind me of that occasion and it never fails to make us all smile. Laughter really is the best medicine.

# "Mums vs daughters = World War 3!"

# EENSIE WEENSIE SPIDER (LIS)

You will no doubt have heard stories of people displaying 'superpowers' when rescuing others, and I have no doubt that these are true, particularly if it is your child who is in danger- adrenaline can do anything! Mums will do anything to protect their offspring, and so it was the day I discovered a massive spider on the lounge room curtain. I, like many people, suffer from arachnophobia, and always rely on my husband to deal with any eight legged creatures that invade our house. Unfortunately, on this particular day, he was still at work and my two boys were sitting on the floor, only a couple of feet from the dreaded nasty. It looked extremely evil and I was totally hypnotised. I contemplated moving to another room, but the fear of coming back and finding it gone put that idea to bed! How was I going to kill it?

I couldn't hit it with a shoe, that would mean getting up close and personal, and it may have dropped and scurried across the floor, something I was not prepared to deal with. I decided that insect spray was my best plan of attack and from a safe distance directed a stream on to its back. Imagine my horror when it reared up, causing me to run screaming from the room. Luckily the boys thought it was a great joke and fell about laughing; I pretended that I too thought it funny, but inwardly I was a quivering mess! Back I went and sprayed again and again; that monster was not going anywhere near my babies! Eventually it curled up and fell to the floor where I proceeded to pound it with a shoe. I'm surprised there were no holes in the floor I hit it so hard and so many times!

If my babies had not been there I would not have done this – I would have gone out until my knight in shining armour came home from work to save the day. Years later there was a *massive* huntsman sitting on the back of my laptop and one of my boys bravely dealt with it with a mixture of spray and a shoe ready for when it dropped from the bench, whilst the other one (who has unfortunately inherited my phobia) and I were busy clutching each other for moral support on the other side of the room as it scurried about! These days, if I find a spider, I call upon my brave boy for help, then retreat to the other side of the room. He just sighs and grabs a shoe to deal with it.

Strangely enough, on our visit to a reptile zoo in Alice Springs, my brave spider killer was hiding with me at the back of the room, safely behind a closed door, whilst his brother had a python draped around his neck!

Go figure- at least my fears are divided between them!

"Put down the shoe... we can talk this out!"

# BOYS WILL BE BOYS (LIS)

When people learned that we had two boys, there was often the comment *"they must be a handful,"* or *"it must be rough and noisy in your house"*. These stereotypical remarks used to annoy me greatly; my boys were mostly quite gentle and I certainly knew plenty of girls their age that were much more of a handful on their own than my two together! People will often gender stereotype, with even parents doing it; often at playgroup I would hear a mum sigh *"boys will be boys"* as they indulgently watched their little horror punch another kid. No punishment would be meted out, just a resigned acceptance that boys will behave like that. No wonder the kids kept doing it! Mine were taught what acceptable behaviour was, and what was not, and I would have done exactly the same if we had two girls!

Later, it was expected that our boys would love football and cricket, and whilst one is good at most sports he tries, (like his Dad), the other hates most sports! He would have rather had extra homework in school than participate in a compulsory sporting activity, and sport was the only thing he disliked about school. Unfortunately for him, there was compulsory Saturday sport at the school they attended, and there he took great pride in losing his tennis matches 6/0! Both his Dad and I are quite competitive and would wonder how this kid, who would happily let the opposition cheat, could be ours! However, try cheating him on a video game, and it's a different matter; he does have a fiercely competitive streak- just not on the sports field!

"His little hands stole my heart and his little feet ran away with it!"

# Race for the Front Seat (Tracey)

Most of us are competitive in some form or another; some extremely so! This is very much the case with kids, often between siblings, creating many headaches for parents. A typical scenario is the race to sit in the front seat of the car; the winner achieving top dog status for the duration of the journey, the loser sulking in the back! This race is taken very seriously by kids with often a standoff result, meaning Mum or Dad is forced to decide; never an easy choice, and guaranteed to end in tears! It sounds such a small problem, but for mum it is a draining start to the day, and can be the equivalent of World War 3!

I decided I would be smart and employ logic; the eldest goes first, and then turns are taken. What a genius idea that was (NOT); now I was faced with having to remember who sat there last, with both claiming it was their turn! Mum, (umpire, manager, role model) gets to decide and deal with the fallout- lucky me!

This occurs throughout your days covering everything from pushing the button at the pedestrian lights to pushing the button for the lift. One thing's for sure- they never hesitated to push my buttons, whether taking it in turns or all at once!

The official rules for calling Shotgun.

1. The shotgunner must be in clear sight of the car and shotgun can be called regardless of whether the driver is in sight of the car.

2. If you are the first to be picked up on a journey, you are automatically given shotgun. You retain this position for the entire journey.

3. You cannot declare shotgun if someone has previously declared shotgun for that journey.

4. When simultaneous shotgun is called, there is then a foot race to the passenger side door from all the people who called."

# PLANES, TRAINS AND AUTOMOBILES (LIS)

Being a mum of little boys means there are lots of trains, planes, buses, trucks and other transport vehicles in your life. My husband was one of four boys, so he certainly knew all about this theme! The boys loved trains so we often went "train spotting", and every year there was a special trip to see the Thomas the Tank Show at Emerald, starring the Fat Controller. It was a truly magical day, one that was also enjoyed by their Pa (a complete train nut!) At home they had a magnificent Thomas Railway set, complete with tunnels, bridges and even Cranky the Crane. Although expensive, the pieces are very durable and after many years of much use, it is now safely packed away (hopefully for future grandkids!) Their favourite episode of Playschool was completely about trains and this was recorded and watched countless times. Often we would sing, *"Going through the tunnel, oh yeah!"*

Many miniature railways have been visited and I must say I really loved those rides cuddled up to my little boys. One train trip that was not so enjoyable was the overnight train in Egypt where it lost power and lurched to a halt. Pitch blackness and voices shouting in a foreign language do not make for happy little boys (or Mum and Dad for that matter)!

Boats too have featured in our travels and I have great and not so good memories of our Whale Watching cruise in New Zealand; the whales were truly magnificent but the ensuing seasickness was not! Other day trips, often with Nanna & Pa in tow, were to Tooradin airport, where we would watch the planes both land and take off, to the docks to watch the ships, including the Spirit of Tasmania, and of course every second year, the big one, The Avalon Air Show. I am quite happy to say that when they were older I was allowed to pass on going! (There are only so many air shows a girl can go to, and quite frankly the only planes I want to see these days are ones that are taking me on holiday!)

Another favourite destination for plane spotting was near Tullamarine Airport, and our family has fondly dubbed this "Geeks' Corner!" Here you will find several cars parked, with all occupants gazing expectedly at the sky for the big incoming silver birds! It's quite breathtaking as they thunder over your head on their downward descent! I think we should have opened a café there; we would have made an absolute fortune! My husband still has a fascination with planes and *every* holiday photo album where we travelled by plane features shots of each plane we went on!

All in all, although I don't appreciate an overload of trains, planes and cars, I'm not a frills and lace sort of girl, so I'm very glad I was blessed with two little boys.

"If planes taxi, how come taxis don't plane?"

# POCKET MONEY (LIS)

The giving of pocket money is an age old dilemma for parents, and one that is not easily resolved. We had various stages where we tried to instigate it, my intention being to reward the boys for completing chores. I thought this would teach them the basic principles of money; you want something enough, you earn money and save for it! The problem was in knowing how much to give, and what they would be expected to buy. Both boys were huge readers and being an avid reader myself, I would never refuse to buy them any books they wanted. We did join the library, but often the books they read were part of a series, and they wanted to collect and keep them. They were totally disinterested in any sense of fashion or shopping when younger, so I bought all clothes for them. Computer games were something they definitely wanted, but expensive to save for, and their birthday was in November, meaning gifts and money were all at one end of the year!

Then there was the great debate-*should they have to earn it*? Should we give them money without expecting anything in return, or should they be paid for various household chores? I believe that doing daily chores is part and parcel of being a family, so I baulked at paying for them to be done, but for a time we had a reward chart on the fridge. Somehow we managed to survive with both boys having an understanding and appreciation for money (especially when we give it to them!).

Money is the core of many parenting issues, ranging from sending them to private school, to how much money the tooth fairy brings. No single rule works for every family, so my advice is to do what works for you, and learn by trial and error!

Reward: For today's wi-fi password.

1) Empty dishwasher

2) Vacuum

3) Walk dog

4) Take rubbish out

# THE WIGGLES CONCERT (TRACEY)

I'm sure you have all heard of The Wiggles, the phenomenally successful performing group, originally consisting of four men, each wearing a different coloured skivvy. Children all over the world have fallen in love with their music and dancing and Kathleen at three was no exception! She was absolutely besotted, singing along to her favourite songs such as "Hot Potato," "Rockabye Bear," "Fruit Salad," "Big Red Car," and lustily bellowing "Wake up Jeff" at the TV.

I was thrilled when I saw they were performing at the Entertainment Centre and then completely devastated when I found it had sold out! I desperately wanted my little girl to see her idols before she outgrew them, so I did some research and discovered they were playing at Geelong, a two hour drive away. I didn't want to travel there without another adult to accompany me so I asked Lis if she would come and happily she agreed. Tickets were purchased and the countdown began!

At last the big day arrived and I don't know who was more excited

– Kathleen or me! After a long drive we reached the venue and found our seats, amongst an army of very excited kids (and mums)! Pandemonium broke out when the first Wiggle, Greg bounced out on to the stage in his yellow skivvy and the music began. Kathleen was spellbound, dancing and singing along, and she had the hand movements down pat.

She looked so adorable I just had to get it on video, even though recording was strictly against the rules. I took my video recorder from my bag and stealthily began taping Kathleen performing "Rockabye Your Bear".

However, unlike the phones that you can use today, there was no hiding the cumbersome recorder I had then, and soon an official came and politely informed me if I didn't stop I would be asked to leave. Happily, I had already managed to capture most of the song.

I am not a rule breaker by nature but sometimes being a mum makes it a necessity and consequently I have a memento from my baby girl's first ever concert!

"I want to sit in the moshpit at the Wiggles concert!"

# THE F BOMB (LIS)

One of many things that I am proud of as a mum is my kids' manners and their lack of swearing. Whilst I am no prude, I really hate hearing the 'f' word overused, especially by kids and often unnecessarily, however when used in context it is a very effective expletive that can convey a lot of feeling!

I vividly remember the day my boys told me (they were in the bath at the time) that they knew what the F word was. They were about six at the time, and having been subjected to the school playground and kids with older siblings, I had no doubt that what they said was true. Imagine my surprise (and amusement) when, after much persuasion tell me, one of them finally blurted out FART! Dutifully I hid my laughter and informed them that wasn't it. Unfortunately both are blessed with my insatiable curiosity and need to know things, and would not let the matter drop. They insisted on knowing what the word was, but for the life of me I couldn't bring myself to say it to those two freshly scrubbed faces gazing up at me! Instead I sidestepped and told them it rhymed with duck and started with F…

moments later after a little thought, out it blurted from one of their mouths!

Many people over the years have complimented me on the boys' good manners, with some telling me how lucky I am. Luck had absolutely nothing to do with this; it was years of "what do you say?" and "what's the magic word?" constantly asked until finally it came naturally without any prompting.

I am proud when they hold the door open for their elders and appreciative of the sarcastic "you're welcome" said to the surly adult who pushes past with no acknowledgement. Many of our elders can learn from our youngsters. It's an arduous task teaching your toddler manners, but it's a worthwhile gift that you give them for life….

"Swearing - because sometimes "gosh darn" and meanie-head just don't cover it!"

*"I hate X#!$%@&#!! Vegetables!"*

# SLEEP (LIS)

Sleep became the most treasured thing in our world once our little bundles of joy arrived. Our whole lives soon revolved around the sleep/feed routine and this seemed to last forever. In the initial stages I think we went from happy, normal people to robotic shells that functioned on autopilot. For me, the rude awakening for the night feeds was by far the most challenging aspect of our new roles as parents.

I am a night owl by nature, so the adjustment to the rule of sleep when you can took some doing. It would seem like you had just drifted into a wonderful dreamy sleep when a mewling cry would pierce your cocoon. No hitting the snooze button and waking up slowly here; it was bang, awake, go, go, go before the battle cry intensified! I'm sure night feeding today with the advent of Foxtel and Netflix, would not be quite as bad with at least there being something decent to watch on the TV. I on the other hand, often felt I was the only person awake in the world, trapped in a world of home shopping with ab machines, exercise bikes and plastic smiles assuring me I could have a fabulous body in weeks! However, there is a downside to having something decent to watch; you would want to see the end of the show instead of putting your now settled baby back to bed! So begins a life of putting your children's needs before yours; and this never ends!

Sleep was the key to happiness and sanity in our world, and we soon learnt different ways to achieve this. By day I would "vacuum" the children to sleep with the gentle whirr of the motor lulling them to sleep. This was fantastic, as it meant our kids learnt to sleep with loud noise around; the drawback was the hole burnt in the floor the time I left the vacuum running without pushing it! The boys certainly went to sleep, but that floor never recovered!

I abandoned the usual practice of putting them down in the cots during the day, instead choosing to let them sleep on the floor in the family room, allowing me to watch over them both, either asleep or awake. They would often intertwine limbs whilst they slept, and as they grew older we pushed the cots together and they would hold hands. I guess they each had their very own living "security blanket" right from the time they were conceived!

One of my boys loved to go to sleep whilst you gently patted him on the bottom; the rhythmic motion seemed to soothe him and soon he would be fast asleep in the land of Nod! That same baby needed to have a ten minute "mummy snuggle" before bed, and if he didn't get it he wouldn't settle!

In the first few weeks, until we established a routine, everything was just a blur. I remember going into their room one night and standing there uncertain which baby it was I had just fed! We soon learnt to write everything down and gradually we settled into a pattern where we knew what we were doing (most of the time). Our kids were pretty good sleepers, albeit early risers and I realised everything was bearable as long as you had enough sleep.

On the weekends in the early days, my husband and I would take a baby each to settle after feeding, and grab a much cherished nap on the couch. Invariably one baby would not settle and the holder of the other would gloat "my baby's the good one- he's asleep!"

We were given a wonderful gift of an electric swing when they were born, and it proved to be worth its weight in gold, particularly when I was on my own. It would be the extra pair of arms that gently rocked one baby to sleep whilst I tended to the other. I believe a consequence of this was my children not being overly fond of swings when we hit the playground. I think they had swung enough to last a lifetime!

Sleep in the car was another challenge with another set of rules. I'm sure all new parents can relate to the game of "roll slowly to the traffic lights, whilst praying for them to change!" Nobody hates a red light as much as the parent of the baby or toddler who has just nodded off due to the motion of the car. You just know that the car stopping will wake them and this can be extremely ugly!

Another favourite memory is the time spent in the car with my boys whilst they slept. If we reached home and they were sound asleep, rather than risk waking them whilst carrying them inside, we would take it in turns to remain in the car, parked in the driveway. Often my wonderful husband would bring me out a cup of coffee and I would have an hour or so of bliss. I'm not quite sure what anyone who walked past the car would have thought, but at that time, I couldn't have cared less!

"If you don't want your nap, can Mummy have it?"

# BELT UP! (TRACEY)

When Millie was 3, she went through a minor rebellious stage. When we went out in the car to go shopping or visiting, Kathleen was old enough to sit with a normal seatbelt; Millie sat in a toddler car seat with a seatbelt, Louise in another beside her. Millie decided she didn't like wearing her seatbelt, it must have been too constricting, and began undoing the clip without me knowing. Eventually I realised that she was doing this, pulled over, refastened the belt and gave her a sermon as to why she needed to keep the seatbelt on. She gazed at me solemnly (eye rolls hadn't occurred to her at this early stage in her life; they came later in her teens). After watching her undo it again in the rear view mirror, I sternly told her if she didn't stop, I would have to take her to the police station and have a policeman talk to her.

I don't think she believed me, and she immediately tested me by unclipping the belt again! I then made a detour to the nearest police station, parked the car and advised the girls we were going in to see a policeman. Kathleen and Millie's eyes went wide - Kathleen's with delight and Millie's with horror! We all approached the counter and I asked the policeman if he could have a serious word with Millie about the importance of keeping her seatbelt on in the car. The young constable gave me a smile and said "sure!" He came and knelt beside Millie and in an extremely authoritative tone explained why she must keep it on. Millie was overawed, by both his size and his uniform.

At the end of his speech he asked her if she would promise to keep her seatbelt on at all times. Millie obediently and very meekly agreed. I smiled and thanked him and he winked in return. Out to the car we trooped where all seat belts were religiously fastened. I look back now and think I should have gone back to that police station for other matters!

"Live for tomorrow, fasten your seatbelt!"

# MEMORIES (LIS)

I am very pleased that I decided to keep many of the notes, cards and letters that my kids have given me over the years. It's guaranteed to bring a smile to my face when I read them. To this day I have the Mother's Day poems that they penned whilst in fourth grade, laminated and hanging on my bedroom wall and I often read them before beginning my day. I also have photo albums filled with their drawings and little notes, one of my all-time favourites being a big red love heart with the words "I love you so much Mummy, I could eat you all up!"

As the years pass by you forget the sweet things they once said, and I believe it's important to preserve these words for later years, when they will warm your heart and bring back long forgotten memories. It's hard to keep a collection of all the paintings and drawings, but a photo taken of each and placed in an album can be kept for a lifetime.

Another gem I kept was a letter from one of our boys begging us not to make him get his hair cut before the special event that was coming up, as it would ruin his life. You will be relieved to know we agreed to his wish, thus saving his life from ruination!

Things that are once consuming and important become buried in the depths of our minds, and it takes a reminder to dust off the cobwebs and bring the memories flooding back!

"100 years from now it won't matter how much money I had, what car I drove or what kind of house I lived in. But the world may be different because I was important in the life of a child."

# MOTHER'S DAY (LIS)

Mother's Day, although tinged with sadness, is a favourite day of mine. I miss my Mum more on this day than others, but I'm lucky to be blessed with a beautiful family of my own that I love very much. My boys were always super excited to give me their gifts and whilst when they were younger all I wanted was a 'sleep in' it was impossible not to melt at the sight of their glowing, excited little faces appearing next to the bed bearing gifts, much needed coffee and gorgeous big cuddles! The week leading up to the day would involve lots of whispering, hiding of parcels and the printer secretly being used. I have quite a collection of gifts from Mother's Day stalls and things made at school and I still treasure each and every one, even more than the more expensive gifts that I receive now. There is so much love in the handmade clay pots and the carefully chosen coffee mugs and teddy bears. I have a photo album full of cards, drawings and little poems that they wrote and they still bring a tear to my eye. They have both always been very good at expressing themselves, both emotionally and on paper for which I am very grateful.

Whilst I had heard stories from mums telling me their kids requested they be dropped at the street corner rather than being taken to the school gate, mine were always happy to be seen with me, no matter who was around. I think helping at Kinder and later at school played a big part in this. I loved sharing their school life and meeting their friends and they were happy to have me there. Communication is an important part of any relationship and I like to think that my boys would come to me about anything. I shared a very different relationship with my own mum, but I think the ways of parenting change from generation to generation. I hope my kids are lucky enough to be blessed in their future family lives with the same happiness that we have had.

PS. When you read this, kids- I'd like a new car next Mother's Day!

"Mothers hold their children's hand for a while, but their hearts forever."

# DADDY'S LITTLE HELPERS (LIS)

Gone are the days when simple things, like helping dad in the garden, were a fun activity and not a chore. The boys would happily don their little gum boots and trudge about the garden, playing with leaves whilst eagerly waiting for the much loved ride in the wheelbarrow. The screams of delight when dad cornered sharply, almost tipping them out, were music to my ears. They loved to climb trees and help dad with the pruning, each begging a turn with the secateurs and chopping wildly until their little fingers got too sore.

Then they would gather all the leaves and cuttings and pile them in the green bin, hoping to fill it to the brim. If this happened, dad would lift them in with instructions to trample it down and gleefully they would take it in turns, hanging tightly to the sides of the bin and jumping up and down! One occasion we were at Gramps' house, where he, being a builder, was busy renovating. He was taking down a wall between two rooms and to the boys' delight said they could help with the sledgehammer. Although the sledgehammer was almost too heavy for them to lift, they swung valiantly and managed to put some satisfying holes in the wall before their arms wore out.

These days their dad has to almost beg to get them to come outside, let alone partake in activities like helping in the garden! I know he greatly misses having his 'little mates' around. Luckily the dog has taken their place as his gardening companion, but somehow I don't think it's quite the same…

"Anyone can be a father, but it takes someone special to be a daddy."

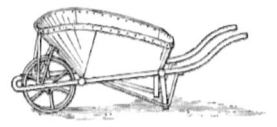

# TV AND DVDS (TRACEY)

Throughout the 1990's, whilst the girls were toddlers, they had many favourite TV shows and movies. Millie loved the Teletubbies and Po was her definite favourite! All my girls loved Rugrats, too. Angelica (there is irony in that name), the oldest, liked to terrorise her cousin Tommy and his friends, and her catch cry of "stupid babies!" was often heard in our house. The Wild Thornberry's was another comedy animated series that the girls loved; they would have given anything to have Eliza's ability to talk to animals.

They also repeatedly watched "The Land Before Time", following the adventures of Littlefoot, Cera, Petrie, Ducky and Spike, dinosaurs who embarked on many adventures every day. Pokémon was a daily viewing and playing with the balls from the show was a common occurrence. Sailor Moon and The Powerpuff Girls were also favourites, and I particularly liked that these superheroes were all female. You have to love girl power!

All of these shows and many others, including Playschool, Bananas in Pyjamas, Blues Clues, Sesame Street and Art Attack, all taught the girls morals and life lessons and generally showed that good will win over evil. I enjoyed these shows almost as much as my girls and am grateful for the entertainment, happiness and valuable lessons that they provided.

"My children's laughter is my favourite sound. The sound of their deep breathing when they are asleep is a close second!"

# TV WORLD (LIS)

Many people will tell you that too much TV is bad for kids and that it is nothing but a convenient babysitter for mums. I personally dispute this and many catchphrases from both TV shows and movies have been used in our house throughout the boys' childhood. I always watched with them and we certainly had our favourite shows. I recently discovered some old videos (yes, it was pre DVDs) on which I had recorded every episode of Rugrats and favourite episodes of Playschool. Many morals were learnt from Rugrats and other such shows. It's strange how kids will watch the same video over and over, never seeming to tire of it and often I could use that as a bribe (oops, I mean reward) to get them to do something.

Dora the Explorer was another favourite and from this we learnt a smattering of Spanish (who knows when you might need that language) and the good old catchphrase "Swiper no Swiping!" which we would yell in unison at the TV. Both boys always needed to know what the title of any episode was and on the odd occasion when I had missed it I quickly learned to make it up to avoid their disappointment. To my amusement they never questioned why "A Day at the Beach" was set in the park! As long as I answered they were happy – if only **that** kept up!

TV, movies, and books all introduce themes and different situations to your kids and are great tools for both communicating and teaching your toddlers (nowadays you would add the internet to the mix). Playschool gave us many activities, things to both do and make; from making playdough to building a cubby house with sheets and chairs. Even as they aged, and Playschool changed to *Doctor Who*, and the shows became more adult and far greater in variety- we still enjoy many of them together as a family.

I think there's always something to learn from TV or movies, and we fostered such a love for this medium, one of my sons studies film and television at university!

"Great mums have sticky floors, messy kitchens; piles of laundry... dirty ovens and happy kids!"

# TROUBLE (LIS)

Kids remember the most random things, often memories that have long since left your mind! Obviously one of my boys was psychologically damaged from the time I shut him in the laundry for misbehaving! No, he was not locked in, he was just too short to reach the door handle, and there was a step down into the laundry. To hear him tell the tale (usually in front of company) you would swear he had been placed in chains in a dungeon swarming with rats! I guess if that was the worst of my punishments, they got off lightly!

I often swore that they would wake up in the morning and decide who was going to be the "good twin" and who the "evil", because for a while they were never both well-behaved at the same time, and you never knew which was going to be which! I vividly remember the time I was *really* angry; they were being especially exasperating and I was chasing them to deliver (horror of horrors) a smack on the bum! Just think how I felt when they both started laughing at me, giggling as they sprinted away! As you can imagine, it did nothing at all to improve my temper!

My other big meltdown came whilst I was helping them with homework. Tension was high and "their listening ears" were definitely not present. With every passing minute my frustration grew until finally I snapped and in a theatrical fashion flung the book across the room! (I can be a bratty kid with the best of them!)

My favourite method was counting to three, me desperately thinking "*oh, crap, three's getting close!*" Luckily for me my boys generally caved at two; or at a push, two and a half! Both boys were angels everywhere they went and with anybody, apart from home and us!

Constantly I was told how good they were and whilst I was appreciative of their public behaviour, I wished they could be angels at home too. But as one put it, "We've been good all day Mum, and you love us no matter what we do." I can't argue with that.

"Children are the only people that can bring you to the brink of insanity and you will still love them tomorrow!"

# WHAT'S THAT SMELL? (TRACEY)

Many years ago an awful odour began to permeate from our study. I searched the room high and low, trying to locate the offensive smell, but to no avail. Days went by with the stench getting stronger. Once more I searched; through drawers and cupboards, on the desk, under the desk, but again found nothing. Finally we decided that a rat or possum must have somehow got trapped in the wall and died, meaning we would have to cut a hole in the wall to try and locate it. Before embarking on this drastic measure I decided I would have one final, thorough search to see if I had missed anything. A small white box that held a tiny glass wishing fairy sat on the desk and when I opened it (thinking the fairy would bring me luck on my search) I nearly passed out. Inside the box sat the shrivelled, rotting remains of a brussel sprout that our younger daughter Millie had put there weeks before, hoping the wishing fairy would make it disappear!

To this day I can't look at one without gagging and remembering the awful stink!

"Do you smell it? That smell. A kind of smelly smell. The smelly smell that smells... smelly!"

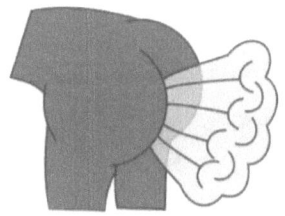

# VENTURING OUT (LIS)

Things can quite often turn out to be very different to what you have envisaged. I was very much looking forward to attending the local Multiple Birth Meeting and was somewhat reticent about attending my Mothers Group, run by the local Council. I couldn't have been more wrong on both counts.

I set off for the Multiple Birth gathering thinking how wonderful it was going to be spending the morning with other mums of multiples, swapping stories and bonding over our adorable babies. Instead I spent the morning listening to the other mums bitch and whine about how hard everything is and nobody understands what it's like to have two. Whilst I agree it is at times very hard, there are always people in harder situations than you, with three or more babies, or even worse with a sick baby. Not only were these mums indulging in a "pity party," they were ignoring the older toddler siblings who were running amok amongst the babies lying on the floor! Add hot cups of tea and coffee to the mix and I was soon on high alert – so much for the relaxing morning. Disappointed and disillusioned, I soon left.

With much trepidation, the next week I headed out to Mothers Group, organised by the local Council and run by a rather scary Health Nurse. It always strikes me as ironic that quite a few professional people running things related to children, have in fact no kids themselves; instead they preach "textbook parenting" to you, which as anyone who has had kids knows, is a fantasy!

A classic example may be as follows; textbook- when your child is having a tantrum, calmly remove them from the room and place in time-out. After a reasonable amount of time, explain in a firm, quiet voice why their behaviour is unacceptable; ask for an apology, and once given return to playing happy families. Reality- child kicks and screams on the floor, not listening to a word you are saying. Eventually you pick them up, getting punched and kicked in the process, and throw them on their bed. After repeating this process several times (they follow you out each time), you eventually scream in frustration "If you come out again, you will not sit down for a week," slam the door for added effect and satisfaction, and exit the room. You then look at the clock and wonder if 11am is too early for a wine!

Whilst this is the extreme case, parenting never goes by the book, no matter how much you want it to. Everyone is different and reacts to situations according to their own personality. My only advice is, if it works for you and your baby, run with it – next week it might not work! But back to Mothers Group; we attended about 8 sessions at the local Health Centre and then started a roster whereby we met at each other's houses. There were seven mums in our group and eight babies with an age gap of about four months from oldest to youngest. It was a mixed group of mums all of whom were lovely, but one mum in particular and I forged an instant bond when we shared eye-rolls over the Health Nurse's comments and have remained friends to this day.

Mothers Group is the first time you encounter "competitive motherhood," whereby you judge and in return are judged, by your baby's behaviour and development. So proud is the mum whose baby first sits unaided, leaving you feeling like a failure and surreptitiously propping things behind your baby until they too reach this milestone! In years to come you realise how ridiculous it all is as eventually all will walk and talk, but at the time it is your yardstick to success. This will continue throughout your life and I expect will carry on to when you have grandchildren!

The greatest thing I got from these outings was much needed adult company and the chance to both gain and to share some invaluable tips from mums who are going through the same things as you.

I vividly remember listening to them complain about their mums (the grandmas) looking after their baby and not doing it right, and thinking how lucky they were to *have* a mum to babysit for them and give them some free time. I watched other babies struggle to feed, or throw up afterwards (dreaded reflux) and count my blessings my two didn't have that problem. Everyone, it was clear, had their own benefits and weaknesses, and everyone was different- we often just don't realise how lucky we are. I learnt to be organised; so much so I was generally first to arrive! I packed the bag the night before, I got dinner prepared before lunch, I laid out bath clothes in the morning – I had a real routine! Most importantly I had a shower and was dressed every morning by 9am, as this made me feel I had achieved "human status" for the day and could face almost anything!

Whilst the majority of mums in our group returned fairly soon to the workforce, my bonded friend and I stayed home with our kids. I have honestly never regretted this decision, and whilst I know for some it is financially impossible, I am grateful I could, and I have (and hope my kids do too) many treasured memories of this time together.

"You know you're a parent when it takes longer to load everyone and everything in to the car than it does to do the actual errand!"

# YARRAM POOL (TRACEY)

On a warm summer's day whilst away at our holiday house, we decided to go for a swim at the nearby town of Yarram at the public swimming pool. Our girls were very excited; Kathleen was 6, Millie 4, and Louise 2. A girlfriend was on her way to the pool to help me with the girls, whilst our husbands were going to arrive a bit later and join in the fun. Kathleen, being the eldest and confident from her recent swimming lessons that she had received the month before at her primary school, decided to race off to the big pool. I watched her hop in the shallow end, which was a meter deep. With her feet touching the bottom, her head was well above the water. I held onto Louise and told Millie to stay near to my side. I had laid our towels and bags down and we were starting to settle. We had the whole pool to ourselves and there were no lifeguards on patrol. I knew that my girlfriend Noelene was about to arrive, and her second set of adults eyes would be very helpful.

I watched Kathleen swim around, and became concerned when she began to swim from one side of the pool in a diagonal direction instead of straight across the 25 metre distance. Because of the angle she was swimming, I knew the depth of the pool was going to be too deep for her to be able to stand up if she had to stop and catch her breath. I yelled out to her, but she couldn't hear me. She swam on and to my horror she stopped to have a rest and tried to stand. Panic set in when she found she couldn't touch the bottom. I was fully clothed and knew I had to act fast. I quickly grabbed Millie's hand and told her to look after Louise. I ran to the pool and jumped in, Kathleen flailing around in the centre of the pool. I reached her very quickly and lifted her up in my arms. She was safe, but her face said it all; she was in shock. I turned to check on the other two and saw they were dumbfounded, by their crazy mum jumping in the pool with her clothes on, including shoes and sunglasses.

I helped Kathleen out of the pool and we all sat quietly on our towels for a short time. Noelene arrived soon after and she could see that I was wet through; it was a truly awful experience. I was so glad that Kathleen was alright, but I think we all learned that day that danger in everyday places like pools isn't an abstract notion; it really is important to keep an eye on your kids by the water.

"You know you're a parent when they fall and the first thing you do is say "You're ok!"

# GOING ONCE, GOING TWICE (LIS)

The boys have lived in our house for almost all their lives and we often tease them that one of them actually bought it at auction! We weren't seriously looking to buy another house, but one evening we stopped to look at one that we had seen in the paper. My husband went in, whilst I waited with the boys, (who were around six months) in the car. Upon returning to the car he said I should go and have a look, knowing full well I would love it with its cathedral ceilings and floor to ceiling windows. I wondered around, loving it, but not getting too excited as we believed it to be out of our price range. Back at the car, one of the boys had decided in his fashion to mark his territory! Out with the change mat, a quick change of the nappy in the boot and we were good to go! The auction was the following Saturday, and we decided to go along just to see what it fetched. We believed it would sell for over $300000 and $285000 was about our mark, so we weren't even expecting to bid.

Jokingly I told my husband he could buy it for Mother's Day (which was the next day) so he threw the chequebook in, 'just in case!' It was a beautiful morning and there was quite a crowd there; the bidding began and to my surprise my husband's hand went up. There were other bidders but eventually it was just us and one other. The auctioneer asked if we wanted to go higher, and one of the boys waved his hand in the air, causing a wave of laughter. We validated his bid, and before we knew it the house was ours! People were clapping; we were just looking at each other in disbelief. I remember going home and ringing my dad, saying "Guess what? – we just brought a house!" We had used the money that my mum had left me and this made it feel like it was her gift to us. It was only six months since she had passed away and it would be hard to move from our present home that had memories of her, but I knew she would love this new house.

For the next couple of months, I would drive the boys to our new neighbourhood and have their afternoon walk, with them in their double pram; I couldn't wait to move in. Many years later we considered moving, but loved both the neighbourhood and the house so we renovated instead. We have so many family memories here, just about all of them- happy, sad, and funny- that when the time comes to move I know it will be a sad day indeed.

"Bricks and mortar make a house, but family love makes a home..."

# THE FAMILY HOME (TRACEY)

When our third daughter came along we decided our house was no longer big enough, and the search for a larger one began. We decided we would prefer a two-story home with bedrooms upstairs and the living areas below. Real estate agents took us through many homes, but none had the character that we sought. I then decided to look at new houses, and after much persuasion from me, Ray agreed to look at display homes; the idea being we would purchase land and build.

Off we went to Hallam with all three girls in tow. Louise was in the pusher with the older two walking beside. There were ten homes to see and the girls were excitedly running around keen to explore each one. We left the pusher at the door of the first home and carried Louise form house to house. All were lovely, complete with beautiful modern fixtures and furniture. However, it was at house number nine that I turned to Ray and told him that it was the one; I loved everything about it. Ray instantly burst my bubble, telling me it was well out of our price range, and when we looked at the price it certainly was. Dejectedly we went to the last home and saw that it was $125 000. Ray informed me if we liked it we could afford it. So in we went, me armed with a camera. I took photo after photo and found I liked the house more and more as we progressed. Just then, Millie ran out of the upstairs master bathroom looking very guilty, Kathleen behind her crowing "Millie broke the towel holder!" Horrified, we went to investigate and sure enough she had broken one end away from the wall. Ray managed to push the screw back in, giving the appearance that all was fine, but one touch and down it would come. Quickly we made our getaway and headed home where after much discussion we finally agreed that we would build our new home.

We purchased a lovely block of land in Lysterfield, sold our home in Upper Ferntree Gully and then rented a home in Rowville whilst our house was built. Six months later, we excitedly moved into our new home; the girls were thrilled to each have their own room. We are currently still living in the same home and have many wonderful, happy memories of the last sixteen years spent here.

Louise, our youngest, is in her last year of school and we are about to enter the next phase of our lives, with retirement creeping ever closer. I would like to spend our future years down on the Mornington Peninsula near the water, but Ray isn't keen! I'm not fazed at all by this- it's normal for him to hate my ideas until they happen and he realises how great they are!

"I want a marriage, not just a wedding,

I want a family, not just a baby,

I want a home, not just a house,

I want a future, not just promises!"

# THE MAGIC OF HARRY POTTER (LIS)

Harry Potter and his magical world have played a huge part in our boys' childhood. The first Harry Potter book was published the year the boys were born, 1997, but it was some eighteen months after that before I had the time to read again! A girlfriend of mine recommended it and once I started, I was hooked.

So it was that I passed my love for the boy with the lightning scar on to my kids. We always read to them every night before bed, and when they got that little bit older we decided to read them Harry Potter. I went to the library and got the audio tapes of the first book and each night we would lie there and listen to the incredible Stephen Fry's reading of the story. With his unique, brilliant character voices we were quickly transported into the wizarding world and many a night the rule of *'just one chapter!'* was broken- more often than not because mum and dad wanted to know what happened next!

My kids were enthralled and would play imaginary games, involving

Ron, Harry and Hermione for hours at a time. Nanna made them wizard capes and we had many costumes, toys, glasses and of course wands. I knitted them scarves, one Gryffindor and one Slytherin, and for their sixth birthday party we went to a Harry Potter puppet show. When the first movie was released, I went with Tracey and Kathleen, her eldest, who was three years older than my two. When the second movie was released, the boys were that bit older and we decided to take them to the drive in where they could sit on our knees and snuggle whilst watching. They loved it, particularly when the flying car soared across the screen. Their rapt expressions on seeing it soar above London will forever be a special memory of mine.

From an early age they devoured the Harry Potter books and both have read each one several times. The movies have been watched so much they can essentially (as can I) recite them word for word. PlayStation games have been played and many an incantation cast under our roof; I remember playing one PlayStation game where the characters were in Gringotts Bank in the mine carts, and I had to help to get the boys past the hard parts (I don't get a turn at all these days!), playing it so much I got motion sickness! I didn't let that stop me, though, and finally I mastered it! (Mummy really was the coolest back then!)

Each year when a new movie was released we would be at the first session, often with the boys dressed up, and usually we would go at least twice. When the final movie came, we booked family tickets to the midnight session (they had pleaded and cajoled with their Dad, who wasn't keen as he had to go to work the next day; saying it had been such a part of their growing up, we just had to go!) and when the music began an eerie hush fell and chills ran down my spine. When it ended, I felt quite sad and empty; a door had closed on a huge chapter in our lives. Thank you to JK Rowling and the boy from the cupboard under the stairs; you bought so much special magic into our lives.

"I solemnly swear that we are up to no good..."

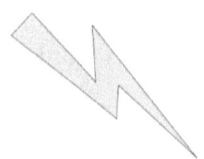

# THE LITTLE THINGS (LIS)

Often in life it is the little things that mean so much and this was definitely true when my boys were toddlers. For a time they had an obsession with the moon and it became a nightly ritual to be held up to look at it (a large sky light and floor to ceiling windows that made this activity easy). Whilst this obsession was in place "The Moon Dance" came into being and this lasted for many months.

Another family ritual was in the summer months waiting for Dad to come home, the three of us perched on our brick letterbox. Each car that turned onto our street, we would say "Is *this* Daddy?" Followed by a groaned, "No, that's not Daddy!" until finally his car turned into our street and they would jump up and down, clapping and waving wildly when he flashed his headlights. There's nothing quite like two adoring faces welcoming you home; it was a definite heart melter for me on the rare occasions when I was the one that had gone out without them!

Helping to wash the dishes was another favourite activity (sad to say they've left that *well behind*!) whereby they would climb on a small chair and gleefully wash the dishes in the soapy water. It certainly made a watery mess, but the smiles were worth it! Then of course there was the world of transport; I would take them to the railway line where we would wave to the train drivers and passengers on passing trains. Trucks and buses were excitedly pointed out on every drive, and last but not least the rubbish truck proved the ultimate excitement. At our beach house we would hear it approaching and would all start yelling "quick, quick it's coming!" and race to the window to watch!

Strangely enough none of these activities cost any money, and yet they remain some of my most treasured memorable moments with our kids!

"When I say "mopped the floor", what I really mean is my kids took a bath, got water everywhere and I wiped it up with a towel!"

# TOYS "R" US (TRACEY)

When Kathleen was four, Ray and I took her to the huge local toy store, Toys 'R' Us. We wandered around looking at the popular toys then; Teletubbies, Tamagotchis, Pokémon, Gameboys, Barney, Rugrats and Blue's Clues to name a few. Kathleen loved Pokémon- her 5th Birthday had a Pokémon/Barbie theme! Kathleen was in her element, racing around enjoying the vibrant colours of all the toys on offer. We were watching her closely and following her from one aisle to the next. However when we turned into the next aisle, she was nowhere to be seen! Gone... I turned to Ray with a look of horror.

I searched the next aisle to no avail. I had a sick feeling of dread in the pit of my stomach; panic was setting in and my mind was racing. Eyes wide with terror we formulated a plan of action. He remained and began searching the area again. I went to the front and scanned the area around me. I yelled to the lady at the customer enquiry counter and asked her to put a call over the store loudspeaker for anyone to find our missing little girl. After what seemed like an interminably long time (probably about five minutes) Ray finally found Kathleen and brought her to me at the front of the store. By that time I was a bumbling, crying mess, fearing the worst; that I had lost my only child. I picked her up in my arms and held her very, very tightly. I was extremely thankful that she had been found safe and sound. Years later, Kathleen recalled this event and told us that she was hiding from us and could hear us yelling and searching for her. She was enjoying our concerned attention. She remembered how upset I had been and how she had then realised it wasn't a fun game to play after all.

It was from this event that I looked into designing an arm gadget called "The Kidfinder," complete with the ability to locate your kids for you.

I even looked into having it patented, but this process proved to be very expensive and I didn't proceed! I'm pleased to report there is a sophisticated version of my Kidfinder available on the market for parents to buy today.

"A worried mum does better detective work than the FBI"

# TRUST (LIES)

Trust is a critical part of any relationship, none more so than between parent and child. It covers everything from keeping the monsters at bay to buying them a treat for good behaviour when promised. Kids are fast learners, and if you continue to break promises they soon learn your words are meaningless. I have always tried to deliver on my promises and like to think I have never lied to my kids (seriously, Santa, The Easter Bunny and The Tooth Fairy don't count!) We taught them from an early age that lying is a far worse sin than any bad behaviour they are trying to cover up, and they will be in more trouble for lying than whatever it was they had done wrong in the first place. This will only work if your reaction to them telling the truth is not frightening, making telling a lie the more pleasant option! They learnt very quickly that it is not okay to lie and we often told them the story of the Boy who Cried Wolf.

They aren't perfect, and I know they would have told white lies (as we all do) but when it mattered I always knew they could be counted on to tell the truth. I had often got into trouble for telling lies as a kid, simply because I went red and looked guilty when accused, even though I was in fact telling the truth! My older sister learnt very quickly how to use this to her advantage, and I was often punished for things she had done. I was always very conscious of this with my boys, but thankfully they never blamed each other!

I remember one of them saying to me that he never lied because somehow I always knew what they had done! I like to think I have built in radar that signals me when something is wrong in my kids' world and try to help, even when sometimes I am powerless.

One melted my heart after ringing to tell me of his problem (which I could do nothing about) saying, "It just makes me feel better when I talk to you about it."

And that's what being a mum is about!

"When your parents accuse you of lying, look them in the eye and say Santa, Tooth Fairy, and Easter Bunny"

# EVERYONE'S A WINNER! (LIS)

Back when the boys were aged about 5, I used to complete and send in various puzzles from different magazines, in the hope of winning a prize. Happily I managed to win several, including $1,000 for a correct cryptic crossword entry! There was often also colouring competitions for the kids, and one day I sent one that the boys had carefully completed using their crayons. To my surprise, a couple of weeks later they received a letter of congratulations, with a Thomas video (DVDs hadn't been invented yet!) and a pack of Crayola Twistables! The boys were thrilled with their spoils and immediately wanted to enter more competitions. I tried to explain to them that they were extremely lucky to have won, but they were having none of that, figuring it was an easy way to get presents.

I decided to let them learn a lesson the hard way, so together they carefully coloured a picture using their new Twistables, filled in the entry form and off we set for the letter box. On the way they were chattering excitedly about what they could win, whilst I was warning them not to be too disappointed when they didn't win anything. They were totally convinced that I was wrong, and when a few weeks later I opened the front door to the delivery man, all hopes of them learning that you can't win all the time flew right out that open door! To my utter amazement, they had won a box full of Bananas in Pyjamas goodies; videos, colouring books, bath mat, books, bubble bath and B1 and B2 soft toys. It was just like Christmas, and yes, you guessed it, several times I heard the words "I told you so!"

Just recently we went to Adelaide for the weekend to celebrate their 18$^{th}$ birthday, where we decided to introduce them to gambling in a casino. We thought it better they experience losing their money with us, but whilst the theory worked at the Pokies where they lost $10 in a matter of minutes, it was a different story at the roulette table, where they began winning!

We left the Casino $250 richer than when we had started, so I don't think it was a very successful lesson on how gambling can eat your money! I hasten to add they were happily stockpiling chips for cashing in, ignoring their Dad's encouragement to bet more, so I take comfort that winning didn't make them lose their heads!

"Everyone's a winner? That is false. If everyone won, then we would all tie!"

# HAVE A BANANA! (LIS)

These days I often hear my own sayings said back to me, and whilst I am pleased the boys obviously have listened and learned over the years, it can prove very frustrating! I will occasionally rant that a certain level of Candy Crush (an addiction of mine) is impossible and can't be done, only to hear from one of the boys, "There's no such word as can't, Mum!" I would always use those words when they were struggling with something, and whilst it generally received the classic eye roll, they would always persevere in their endeavours and triumph! Now, when they later ask if I have passed the level and I say yes, cheerfully crow, "see and you said it couldn't be done!"

You will find when your children hit their teens that they will use all your pet expressions, often just to annoy you! I often say "that's not even remotely funny," and, believe me, it's not when your child is the one saying it to you repeatedly! Another strange expression I use is "That's about as funny as a dead ant!" I have no idea where or why I started using this, but again my boys (and husband) often torment me with it! I wonder if one day these expressions will be adopted by my kids and used on our grandkids! I also say "have a banana" which was one of my mum's idiotic expressions, used when we were ignoring her. I think most families have weird and wonderful sayings that pass from one generation to the next; sadly, the boys assure me they don't think the unfunny dead ant will have much of a legacy!

"Motherhood; the days are long but the years are short....!"

# ODE TO MY LIFE PARTNER (TRACEY)

Some of us are lucky enough to have a partner who shares the joy and hard work of raising your children. From day one he has been an integral, ever supportive part of raising our girls. He has always worked full time, and on top of this was always ready to lend a hand with nappy changes, feeding, holding, burping, washing, playing- anything that needed doing! On more than one occasion I remember saying to him when he arrived home from work "thank god you're home, I'm exhausted!" It has been a joy to watch him over the years interacting with them, making them laugh and opening their eyes to the world in a very humorous way. As the kids grew older and more inquisitive, they asked many questions, and I remember the constant question he was always being asked when working on something- "What are you doing, Dad?"

Without missing a beat, he would always come back with "Well darling, I'm underwater ark-welding of course!" They would look at him with wide confused eyes, not understanding what he was saying and meaning at all. If I was around I would butt in and explain what their father was really doing (making a chicken house, or whatever it was at the time). I'm not sure what age they were when they realised and actually understood what he was saying, but they find it funny now! They often asked him who people were, whether on the TV or down the street if he waved at someone. He would always say, "Oh, that's Fred!" It wasn't, of course- he had no idea what their name was, but he even if it was a woman, he would say that it was Fred (periodically Frederica). Now they know if they ask who someone is, that they will invariably be told their name is Fred. Another common saying I have heard him mumbling to them over the years is "should be happy to do." It is usually said when he mixes up his words and realises he's not making any sense, so decides to make sense of it to himself by saying "should be happy to do" and walking off from the conversation.

The girls all love their father's unique sense of humour and I am sure they have all inherited a piece of it from him. He has made all of our lives special and fun on a daily basis and I feel so lucky to have him in our lives.

"I love being married to my best friend. I can tell him anything, because half the time he does not hear me!"

# REVENGE TIME (LIS)

When the boys were toddlers, I was forever saying "just a minute, mate!" I only have one pair of hands, and I had two little boys to deal with! I often used to jokingly comment that their first words would be "in a minute" as they had heard it so often, but I am happy to say "*Mum!*" was the first spoken word! From an early age both boys were big talkers and would parrot both all they heard and saw, often causing much laughter. I would have my first sip of coffee for the day, followed by a long satisfied *aaahhhh,* and before long the boys began to copy, sucking on their bottle followed by their own *aaahhhh*; it never failed to put a smile on my face!

The tables turned however, from about age 14 onwards, and revenge was theirs! Each time I would ask for something to be done, or tell them that dinner was on the table, back would come the reply; "*in a minute*" from the other room, and this has continued to this day! At least I had a good reason for making them wait; I was tending to their sibling! I'm sure that they will argue that their messaging and games are equally legitimate reasons, but I beg to differ!

"When your mum says: "Just a minute...."

# ME, MYSELF, I (LIS)

I am well known amongst my friends for being pedantic about spelling and grammar, and this is something I am proud to say that I have passed on to my kids. My reputation is such that when we are playing Boggle at our holiday house with friends, I am (quite rudely) banned from playing! When doing the crossword as a group, again I am not permitted to answer until everyone else has had a chance. What can I say? Words are just "my thing!"

Both boys have followed in my footsteps; the first word one learnt to spell was BALLOON – no cat or dog for him! They love, and always have loved, reading, and I believe this was invaluable in making them prolific spellers. My Dad (Gramps) is very proud of his grandsons' academic achievements and is always looking for ways to trick them. One of his favourite (and well told) anecdotes tells of when he asked one of them to spell the word 'to' (too, two). He happily chortles and says, "He got a high distinction in a spelling exam and yet it took him three times to spell that simple word!" I cannot tell you how many times we have heard that story and yet

Gramps never gets an eye-roll! (That is saved for Dad and me!)

I was often helping in the classroom at school and would always correct whoever and *me* to whoever and *I*; I was very much a broken record, but imagine my delight when I heard the kids correcting each other whilst we were away on Camp! This has also happened with the boys' friends (hang around me long enough and it starts to rub off)!

I like to think I'm doing my little bit to keep the Grammar Gods happy!

Look at what a comma can do.

Let's eat Grandpa...

Let's eat, Grandpa.

# FAMILY HOLIDAYS (LIS)

We are lucky enough to have enjoyed numerous family holidays in various parts of the world, and these have provided a treasure chest of memories to last a lifetime. The boys certainly took advantage of their experiences, both having wonderful world and geographic knowledge. We have travelled by train, plane, jeep, and bus, and also hired camper vans. The first of our campervan holidays was from Darwin to Alice Springs, and whilst I was secretly dreading the thought of us being in such close proximity for nearly three weeks and all that could go wrong, it proved to be one of our best ever holidays and consequently led to us later hiring one in New Zealand.

Each holiday has provided a myriad of memories, often involving humour from language barriers! We often laugh about my husband's attempts at using Swahili, in particular the occasion when he told the waiter our meal was "Kubwa". The waiters spent some time laughing and pointing before explaining that *Kubwa*, whilst translating to 'great,' refers to great in size, not fantastic! The boys and I found this hysterical, and to this day tease Dad about *Kubwa*. Things quite often get lost in translation, or you pronounce a word slightly wrong and the meaning changes dramatically. So it was on the day my husband thought he was yelling "no!" at the taxi driver who was relentlessly pursuing us trying to get a fare. In actual fact, he was yelling "thank you," inspiring the taxi driver to follow us further! We often laugh about that now, but at the time we were all extremely hot and bothered (Zanzibar is one of the hottest places we have ever been) and it wasn't that funny. The boys also tease me mercilessly about my pronunciation of the word *Bahn Hof* (station) whilst we were in Germany. Apparently I said it with a very Australian accent which the boys found endlessly funny. I, strangely enough, didn't find it particularly amusing, and still don't when they tease me about it now!

I was always surprised by people asking whether we were taking the kids with us on holidays; in our eyes it was a given, we were a family, and where we went the kids came. Neither of us could imagine going without them and although we travelled by ourselves to Vietnam whilst they were in China for five weeks with school, it was very strange not having them there. Now they are adults, at university, and doing their own thing; we'll have to get used to travelling on our own. In a couple of months we are off to Sri Lanka, and whilst it is definitely far cheaper travelling without our boys, we know we'll miss having them with us!

"The world is a book, and those who do not travel, read only one page..."

# THE ANZAC ON THE WALL (TRACEY)

My husband Ray has always been interested in learning about the war and honouring Anzacs, and is very keen to pass his knowledge on to our girls. When Louise was about 8, Ray decided to memorise a war poem which had moved him greatly when he heard it on the radio. It is written by a journalist who travelled to Gallipoli to cover the 90th Anniversary of the Anzac landing, and when there was given a box of letters that had been written to and from the war front. These letters inspired him to pen the patriotic poem, "The Anzac on the Wall. "

Ray decided that both he and Louise would memorise the poem, by no means an easy task, as it is quite long. Time after time Louise repeated the lines after Ray, until eventually she could stand and recite it on her own. Each time we watched her deliver it to an audience we were extremely proud, and even now, at age 17, she can recite the words of this special poem without missing a beat. I like to think that one day she will pass this legacy on to her children, just as her father has to her.

# "Anzac Day – Lest We Forget!"

# GOOD GUYS DON'T ALWAYS WIN (LIS)

The teaching of good manners is one of the most important roles of a parent, and whilst I am proud to say my boys (for the most part) have exemplary manners, strangely enough this did cause me some grief throughout their childhood. Any time when there was a crowd of people or kids wanting to see or do something, mine would get pushed and shoved to the back and would be too polite to shove back! It is extremely distressing (and frustrating) as a mum, to see your kids looking helplessly back at you whilst they get pushed aside; sometimes it took all my restraint to stop myself going in to battle for them. It did however teach them that nice guys don't always win, and they also experienced this in their younger school years. It always seemed that the naughty kids that would get a certificate in assembly first (with the teachers believing this would inspire them to behave better) while the good kids were left until last. In class the naughty kid would be rewarded for good behaviour whilst those who always behaved (including mine) would get nothing!

They were learning the hard way that the world is not always a fair place. I could not believe my ears at a School Council meeting when the suggestion was made that a reward be given to those kids who had constantly been late, and then managed to arrive on time for a few consecutive days. They were quite nonplussed when I angrily asked how they thought the kids who had *never* been late would feel, replying that they hadn't thought of that! I think sometimes common sense is sadly lacking, with the focus being one thing; no one thinks to look at the bigger picture, and the impact their actions will have on others.

Happily, despite this, my kids continued to behave well. They had (and still do) a very strong sense of what is right and what is wrong and are not afraid to speak out. When they were younger this was at times a bit awkward; they would loudly point out any wrong doings, oblivious of the fact that the unsavoury looking character who had just littered might not look too kindly on having the error of their ways pointed out. In their eyes it was wrong and I couldn't argue with that. It's a sad fact that in this world today you have to often refrain from correcting bad behaviour; the consequences can be dire. You only have to read the paper, or turn on the news to see multiple cases of retaliation and innocent people being attacked. I constantly told my boys to just worry about their own behaviour; in fact, one of my standard lines was "I don't care what so and so said or did- I'm just interested in what YOU said or did." But, as Edmund Burke said- *"all it takes for evil to prevail in this world is for good men to do nothing."* The boys are smart, and would only do something the best and most righteous, safe way possible, but I think I can honestly say I have raised good men.

"A man who treats a woman like a princess is proof that he has been raised by a queen!"

# THE CIRCLE GAME (TRACEY)

When our girls were all in their teens, we travelled to Europe for a holiday and loved experiencing different scenery and cultures. We mostly journeyed by train, finding it the most economical and stress free way to travel between countries. To help pass the time on our travels we often played a game that the girls had once seen on a TV show, "Malcolm in The Middle". It involved forming a circle with your thumb and forefinger and holding it anywhere below waist height. The object of the game was to coax your "victim" into looking at your circled fingers. Victory was yours if they did, and your reward was to punch them softly on the arm! It entailed being very sneaky and quite creative.

Of course mum and dad were the favourite targets, and the girls took great satisfaction whenever either of us was caught out. It is hard not to look when you are told there is chewing gum on your shoe or money on the ground and several times we were caught off guard. There was much laughter whenever a victim was caught out and I'm sure many foreigners had our family pegged as "mad tourists!" It is often the simple games such as this that give you the most pleasure, creating wonderful memories of special family times that will last a lifetime.

"Laugh often, laugh much, and teach your children to laugh with you"

# FIFTEEN MINUTES OF FAME (LIS)

The one occasion that the boys were late for school was for a very good reason. My husband's brother is a photographer, and does work for Holden Cars, and they had asked if he knew of any 6 or 7 year olds that could be photographed for the research project that they were carrying out in conjunction with Monash University Accident Research centre. This project focused on the importance of restraining children between the age of 5 and 10 in child booster seats until the adult seat belt fit them correctly. My husband and I thought it was a worthy reason to take the boys out of school for the morning, so off we set to the photo shoot. It was a much bigger deal than we had anticipated and imagine our surprise when we saw an actual news crew in attendance! A well-known reporter, Charles Slade, came across to my husband and me and questioned me on how I felt about booster seats, given I now knew research had proven their use helped to prevent or lessen serious injury to children in a crash.

Somehow I managed to answer coherently and then, to my horror, was told it was going to be one of the lead segments on National Nine News that night! I had made sure that the boys looked good for their "photo shoot"- if I'd known I was going to be on camera I would certainly have made more of an effort with my clothes, hair and makeup! Sure enough, that night there we were, large as life on the news. It's amazing how many people saw us and sent messages; we felt quite the celebrity family for a few days. Just last year a portion of the segment was again aired, but I must say my little boys don't look quite the same these days! The boys also had their photo in the Herald Sun which ran an article on child safety in cars, and I confess we bought multiple copies of the newspaper that day!

The boys had other photos published in magazines, one very cute one of them dressed as Buzz and Woody, one with their friend and another with me in New Idea who ran a competition on what it was like to be a new mum. I submitted a photo and wrote a brief poem about being a new mum and this was published next to our picture.

Our photo was the largest on the page!

My entry read;

*"No refunds here- they're mine to keep.*

*What I'd do to get some sleep!*

*Feeling inadequate; like a dummy.*

*Ultimate reward, hearing "Love you Mummy!"*

Another moment of fame was when Daniel (then age 7) was presented with a chocolate mud cake on our flight to London! To this day we don't know why, and found it extremely peculiar, given we had a stopover in Dubai, that he be presented with a cake. It did make it to our Aunt's house in London, a bit squished, but nonetheless yummy!

And these I believe, constitute our fifteen minutes of fame…

"Sorry, your 15 minutes of fame have been used up. Please go back to nowhere!"

# BLAST OFF (LIS)

Over the years we have made many purchases at the Australian Geographic shop; everything from make it yourself volcanoes, robot kits and scientific experiments to assorted flying objects including remote control helicopters and various types of rockets. One such purchase was a rocket whose instructions claimed it would fly 300 ft in the air once a mixture of vinegar and bicarbonate soda was placed in its base.

Excitedly we took it to our beach house and planned the big launch with family friends that had joined us for the weekend. The local footy oval was deemed to be the perfect launching pad, so off we all set. Once there, to our disappointment we discovered we did not have the required amount of vinegar. An emergency dash to the general store where we bought a litre bottle of vinegar, and once again we were set to go!

Carefully the two dads added the ingredients to the base whilst the mums and kids retreated a safe distance away. All eyes were glued to the rocket as the dads also stepped back to safety. Moments passed whilst we all held our breath... 5, 4, 3, 2, 1, .......nothing.

Puzzled, the men went to investigate, bending down closely to peer at the base's contents. That precise moment the mixture bubbled and the rocket shot in the air, causing the men to fall over in their panic to get out of its way.

Meanwhile the rest of us collapsed in hysterics! The rocket flight may have failed, having only shot about 20 ft in the air, but the entertainment that moment of hilarity provided, more than made up for its lack of flying ability. For the remainder of the weekend, every time I, my girlfriend or one of the kids mentioned it, the laughter would begin anew. If we hadn't been laughing so hard, we would have recorded it on our phones and had an instant YouTube sensation!

I have many more memories of remote control helicopter flights and glider planes, especially the one where my husband flew a helicopter into one of the lights above our pool table, causing it to explode! (It had been deemed too windy outside so he decided an indoor flight was in order.) When we went to the light shop to replace it we actually purchased a spare just in case!

You just have to love boys and their toys… (Especially big boys!)

"Houston, we have a problem!"

# VISITING LORRAINE'S HOUSE (TRACEY)

One day in 2004, Ray and I needed to visit Lorraine, a work colleague/friend of mine. She lives in the same neighbourhood, so we didn't have far to travel. It was going to be a quick visit, just to drop something off, so we took our girls with us. Lorraine greeted us at the door with a beaming, welcoming smile and ushered us inside. She gave us a cup of tea and then showed us around her lovely home. Like us, she had tiled flooring. As we wandered from room to room admiring her interior decor and wide expanse of flooring, Millie (aged 8) exclaimed at the top of her voice, "MUM!!! LOOK AT HOW CLEAN THESE TILES ARE!" Clearly, my tile cleaning wasn't as adequate for Millie as Lorraine's was. Probably not surprising; with three young girls, our floor was constantly subjected to dropped food, crafty bits and pieces and all kinds of other matter! Millie's young 20/20 vision was overwhelmed by this sparkling cleanliness. My face burned with embarrassment, but Lorraine found Millie's comment extremely amusing, so we all had a good laugh. Over the years Lorraine and I have often laughed about this day, but I am sure

Lorraine's tiles are still a lot cleaner than mine are, even though I no longer have small children to blame! Kids will often unwittingly embarrass you with their innocent honesty.

"Wow honey, the tiles are so clean! Was the internet down for awhile today?"

All good things must come to an end and, sadly, this is where we leave you. Whilst we both have countless more memories, at some point we must stop! Perhaps in years to come there will be a sequel – "Nanna's the Word!" - But that is a chapter in both our lives that is yet to be written.

We hope that you have enjoyed reading our memories as much as we enjoyed recounting them, and we wish you much happiness as you create your own memories with your kids.

Lis & Tracey

"There are two times when parenting is the most difficult; when the baby first comes, then when the adult first leaves home..."

www.ingramcontent.com/pod-product-compliance
Lightning Source LLC
Chambersburg PA
CBHW021123300426
44113CB00006B/265